CW01662553

"God's Plans Were Better" is a modern-day, real-life undeniable journal of a believer who has seen and experienced the awesomeness of God's sovereignty and the mysterious nature of His providential care. It offers hope and encouragement amidst a world of uncertainties, tragedies, and problems.

Rev. Dr. Pat P. Glasgow, Ed.D.

Former President of the West Indies School of Theology, Trinidad and Tobago; Pastor, and Author of "*Traversing 21st Century Pitfalls*".

Ann Marie Dewar's "God's Plans Were Better" is an honest, inspiring, and deeply moving personal story – a testament to the certainty of God's benevolent and sovereign guidance in the lives of His children.

Blondina Howes-Jeffrey, M.Phil, M.A. (Ed)

Businesswoman, Retired Educator and Author of "*God Never Says Oops*" and "*When The Brook Dries Up*".

In a world that is experiencing troublesome times, this book is a timely intervention. God's Plans Were Better, as a testimony of personal experiences, engenders hope, whether interpreted in a realm of spirituality or construed on a plateau of agnosticism. Herein lies the power of Divine Providence. I am moved by the author's varied experiences, and the scriptural references that ably support the thread that runs through the narrative.

Dr Gertrude R. Shotte, Ph.D
Director of Studies, Business School, Middlesex University, London, UK; Author of "*Education, Migration and Identities: Relocated Montserratian Students at the Crossroads*" and "*Behind Every Cloud*".

Ann Marie Dewar shares her life journey in this captivating memoir, weaving past and present events with grace and skill. She draws on scriptures to illuminate her experiences and inspire the reader. This is a well-written and powerful book by a gifted storyteller.

Nerissa Golden
CEO of Goldenmedia LLC., and Author of "*Start, Grow, Thrive: Build a Business to Last*", "*Island Days*" and "*Ordained For This*".

GOD'S PLANS were Better

May faith arise as you read this book!

God bless.

Ann Marie Dewar

August, 2024

Also by Ann Marie Dewar

Wha Marmie Say: Poems in the Montserratian Creole Language

GOD'S PLANS were Better

A Personal Witness to
Divine Providence

ANN MARIE DEWAR

ADELINN PUBLISHING
Salem, Montserrat

GOD'S PLANS WERE BETTER

© 2024 Ann Marie Dewar

ISBN: 978-976-97193-1-6

All rights reserved. No part of this publication may be reproduced or transmitted in any form without the prior written permission of the author, except for brief quotations in printed reviews.

Adelinn Publishing
P.O. Box S18, Salem, Montserrat
Email: adelinnpublishing185@gmail.com

Cover design: Goldenmedia
Formatting by BambuSparks
Author Photograph by Ian Gerald

Scripture quotations marked ESV are taken from the Holy Bible, English Standard Version, copyright © 2001 by Crossway, a publishing ministry of Good News Publishers. Used by permission. All rights reserved.

Scripture quotations marked NKJV are taken from the Holy Bible, New King James Version, copyright © 1982 by Thomas Nelson Inc. Used by permission. All rights reserved.

Scripture quotations marked NLT are taken from the Holy Bible, New Living Translation, copyright © 1996. Used by permission of Tyndale House Publishers, Inc., Wheaton, Illinois 60189. All rights reserved.

Disclaimer: Portions of Chapter One were published earlier as part of an online article by Golden, N. "Perfect Timing: How Myron Rolle's Caribbean Neurosurgery Foundation Helped Montserrat's Ann Marie Dewar", *Discover Montserrat*, 01 August, 2022, https://discovermni.com/2022/08/01/perfect-timing-caribbean-neurosurgery-foundation-helped-montserrats-ann-marie-dewar/

For my nephew, Kriston
whose faith inspires me

"Many are the plans in the mind of a man,
but it is the purpose of the Lord that will stand."
Proverbs 19:21 (ESV)

CONTENTS

PREFACE

The term "Divine Providence" as used throughout this book, refers to the wise, loving, authoritative guidance and continuous sovereign care and direction of God. It acknowledges that God has absolute authority over all events in the universe, and in the lives of His creation, so that His purposes may be fulfilled, for our good, and for His glory. No situation or circumstance is beyond God's care and precise direction. According to Holy Scripture, the entire universe, the laws and events of nature, and the environment in which we live, are under His authority (Psalm 103:19; Isaiah 40:26). So too are all the governments and nations of the world (2 Chronicles 20:4-6; Psalm 66:7; Daniel 4:17). Indeed, our lives are in His hands (Luke 1:52; Galatians 1:15), and his loving care for His people is clearly established in Psalm 4:6, Luke 12:7, and many other verses.[1] As Jerry Bridges explains in his excellent book *Trusting God*, "God in His love always wills what is best for us. In His wisdom He always knows what is best, and in His sovereignty, He has the power to bring it about."[2]

We can all probably tell of instances when several related things happened at or near the same time, usually in a way that was unlikely or unexpected. Very often these are referred to as being by chance or coincidence, serendipitous or fortuitous, without any attribution to the sovereignty or purposes of God. Sometimes the significance of these events is not immediately apparent, but the inter-connectedness becomes meaningful in hindsight. The events or situations may happen over time, but uncannily bring about circumstances that resolve issues or problems which we are facing, in a way that was not planned or even foreseen.

Sometimes these situations are major life-altering circumstances, that have the potential to hugely impact one's life and future. Others are not of such great significance, yet can change one's perspective, hopes and dreams and even shake one's confidence. Often, seemingly insignificant situations can have important outcomes.

I have experienced several of these situations throughout my life, and I reflect on some of them in this book. In each case, there was an issue or circumstance which needed to be addressed. Some of these were long-term, like dealing with chronic feelings of inadequacy and inferiority, learning to respond more appropriately to disappointments, or needing to prepare adequately for retirement. Others were shorter term, including sickness, (un)employment, or moments of stress. In many cases, a separate incident or circumstance occurred (often completely unexpectedly), which impacted the situation and provided a resolution.

Whether small teachable moments, or massively impactful (sometimes crushing) life-changing situations, as a Christian believer, I have learned not to downplay these occurrences in life. Rather, on reflection, I now understand them as part of the out-workings of a wise, omniscient, benevolent, and responsive Mastermind of the universe for whom no situation or circumstance is unimportant, and whose generous providence treats with even the minutiae of life.

What is the basis of this belief? Well, it is completely grounded in the Holy Scriptures, which attests to this truth over and over, under both the old and new covenants of God with His people. His sovereignty, care, concern, and direction over every aspect of our lives are all made plain in several promises, declarations, and admonitions. For example, Jeremiah 29:11 - *"For I know the plans I have for you, declares the LORD, plans for welfare and not for evil, to give you a future and a hope"* (ESV) - establishes the principle that God has a plan for each of our lives.

Furthermore, as Proverbs 19:21 makes clear, *"many are the plans in the mind of a man, but it is the purpose of the Lord that will stand" (ESV)*. His plans for our lives cannot be thwarted. And God's loving care for us is shown in Luke 12:7 *"Why, even the hairs of your head are all numbered. Fear not; you are of more value than many sparrows"* (ESV).

I understand, therefore, that God's provisions are not the result of coincidence, but of Divine planning and purpose. So, I do not believe in coincidences. I believe in God, who plans my life from beginning to end, so that circumstances, situations, events, and experiences - emotionally, mentally, physically, and environmentally - happen on purpose and by Divine order and providence. In hindsight, I recognise that I have been given truly outstanding and amazing opportunities to witness the wonder of God's power working on my behalf, and on behalf of others. There is no doubt whatsoever in my mind that God was, and continues to be, at work in every area of my life.

However, nowhere are we promised that God's plans and purposes will keep us from the challenges and problems of life. Quite the reverse! It was Job who uttered these profound words out of his experience of suffering, "*Shall we indeed accept good from God, and shall we not accept adversity?* (Job 2: 10, NKJV) We are, in fact, promised that we will face difficulties, and in this book, there are reflections on a few of these that have occurred in my life.

As many people have found, some of these disappointments and difficult situations will loom large and threaten to overwhelm us. But we are also assured that light will be found at the end of the tunnel. Clouds will have silver linings. We can emerge stronger in faith and richer in character. Simply because, as Romans 8:28 informs us, "... *we know that for those who love God all things work together for good, for those who are called according to his purpose.*" (ESV)

As I look back and reflect on the various stages and pivotal moments of my life, I have come to a new understanding of Divine Providence. As God moved in my life, working out His plans on my behalf, I was usually completely unaware of His action until He was ready to reveal it in His perfect timing. Sometimes that perfect timing was just a few days later, but sometimes it was years, or even decades later. When revealed, I could see, in hindsight, various signs – whether circumstances, something said here or there, or some other indication – which pointed to the hand of God intervening, mobilising people, events, or unexpected encounters, until the action on my behalf was complete.

What a supremely marvellous, limitless, and gracious God we serve! Indeed, as Job 11:7 (ESV) asked, "*Can you find out the deep things of God? Can you find out the limit of the Almighty?*"

John Calvin, the French Protestant Reformer, observed in his *Commentary on the Psalms,* "The whole world is a theatre for the display of the Divine goodness, wisdom, justice, and power ..."[3] From my little corner of the world, I say "Amen!"

CHAPTER ONE

A Runny Nose!

Everyone has had a runny nose at some time. Most of us have had more than one episode of the common cold or influenza. Many persons experience periodic or seasonal allergy attacks, which have brought on a runny nose, sometimes accompanied by sneezing or nasal congestion. I can recall several instances of a slightly runny nose caused by eating spicy food, or going outside in very cold weather. Our bodies, "fearfully and wonderfully made" (Psalm 139:14), respond to conditions which cause irritation and inflammation in the lining of the nose, by producing a clear mucus discharge to try to reduce the irritation or clear the infection.

However, in my case, a runny nose was not a significant symptom of a cold or flu since I had suffered from 'postnasal drip' for decades. This condition causes most of the mucus from the nose to drip down the back of the throat. Hence, I usually only realised I had a cold when I experienced other symptoms like a sore throat, or achy sinuses. After a while, severe coughing episodes would occur (especially at night) as I tried to bring up the excess mucus that felt as if it were lodged securely somewhere in my respiratory tract. On a few occasions this condition had become serious. The challenges of the British climate (which my mother described as "three months' winter and nine months' bad weather") had badly exacerbated my condition, with almost monthly attacks of bronchitis. It was one of the reasons why, in 1991, I knew that the time had come for me to leave London after eleven years, and return to Montserrat, my small island home in the Eastern Caribbean. There, the tropical climate improved my respiratory health considerably.

So when, on a bright and beautiful Monday morning at the end of March 2022, my nose suddenly started dripping, it felt strange. I had awoken feeling fine, done a few chores, then sat down in my favourite and well-worn armchair. Spatially, this is my comfort zone, where I regularly read, pray, watch television, chat with visiting friends, grade students' assignments, peel vegetables, and do hand-sewing. Just after nine o'clock on this morning, I was sitting and reading when I felt fluid dripping from my right nostril. I had no symptoms of a cold, no headache, no sore throat, no nasal congestion or itchiness.

Another drip. This time, it dropped onto the page I was reading. I got up, fetched a paper towel, wiped my nose and tried to continue reading. Drip, drip, drip. Every four or five seconds like a leaking tap, and only from my right nostril. The fluid, clear and runny like water, dripped onto my clothes, and when I stood up, it dripped onto the floor. Very concerned by now, I got up and went to the bathroom, and looked in the large mirror over the sink. The dripping continued, but now I could see it. It was not a pleasant sight, and it truly frightened me.

The seasoned researcher in me flew into action. I picked up my smartphone, googled "what causes runny nose," and clicked on the websites of a few internationally renowned medical institutions. The usual information about colds, flu, irritants, and allergies was all there, and suggested that most cases of runny nose were not serious and would go away, especially if helped by taking decongestants.

However, most of the sources also mentioned a few rare, but quite serious, conditions which would lead to a runny nose. Two conditions were explained. One of these did not match my symptoms at all. But the other was called "cerebrospinal fluid (CSF) leak," and when I read the entries the information increased my heart rate. As a high school and college Biology teacher, I understood what cerebrospinal fluid is. It is a clear, watery fluid that surrounds the brain and spinal cord, cushioning them from injury, providing them with essential nutrients, and removing waste substances.

From my swift Internet search, I now learned that CSF could leak through a hole in the dura, which is the outermost layer of the membranes (the meninges) surrounding the brain. This hole, or tear, could be caused by severe head trauma, certain types of surgical interventions, or even (rarely) spontaneously, in which case the fluid can escape through the nose or ear.[4] I also learned that loss of cerebrospinal fluid can put too much pressure on the lower sections of the brain, as the brain sinks lower down in the skull, a condition called intracranial hypotension.[5] The risk of infection leading to meningitis, a potentially fatal condition, was also mentioned.

My anxiety surged when I read that in the case of cranial CSF leakage through the nose, the dripping usually occurred from one nostril only. Although I am not a doctor, the possibility seemed strong that the fluid dripping from my right nostril was CSF, which belonged inside my skull, and not on the printed page in front of me.

I phoned my doctor, who was, thankfully, at the hospital, attending to patients in the Casualty Department. She took my call and listened as I tried to explain my symptoms. She asked me to come to the hospital as soon as possible.

The COVID-19 pandemic was in full swing globally, and cases were on the rise in Montserrat. There was a national mask-wearing mandate for entry to all business places and facilities, especially the hospital. By this time, I found that the paper towels I was using to wipe my nose were quickly saturated. So, I unrolled a couple of sheets of paper towels, and folded them to make a pad which I put over my right nostril, inside my mask. I took a few more just in case and drove myself to the hospital. I prayed, with some desperation, and delivered my situation to God, asking for His intervention according to His will.

My doctor has a bubbly personality, and is one of the most caring physicians I know. As she greeted me at the hospital and saw my condition, a look of sheer concern was evident even through the surgical mask she wore, and I was struck by the stark reality of the situation. My online research had suggested that the more severe (but, I considered, more probable) causes of my dripping nostril were rare. I mentally assessed the medical landscape.

Montserrat is a tiny island with a basic health care system. There were no MRI or CT scan machines on the island at that time, and no neurological services. The closest available machines were in neighbouring Antigua. If treatment required the intervention of a neurological practitioner, Antigua was served by an offshore neurosurgeon who visited periodically. Match a rare neurological condition with a small hospital serving a small population, and it was even likely that the few doctors practicing in Montserrat had never seen, let alone managed, the kind of condition I was presenting. It was clear to me that I could be in trouble.

I left the hospital armed with antibiotics, and instructions to monitor the dripping over the next day or two. I was to restrict movements to try and control the flow, and to contact the doctor in case of any dizziness, nausea, headaches, or any other flu-like symptoms.

I drove home and rested. I followed the doctor's orders. The dripping from my right nostril continued. I soaked many sheets of paper towels, until I discovered that lying on my back slowed, but did not stop, the dripping. I have never slept well lying flat on my back but managed to catnap fitfully through the night. Early the next morning, I had a telephone call from my doctor.

"We have consulted with specialists overseas, and we want you to come back to the hospital," she said. "We want to collect some of the dripping fluid for testing."

After assuring her that I was able to get to the hospital, I hung up and got myself together, folding paper napkins to pad my mask as I had the day before.

After the sample collection at the Casualty Department, my doctor dropped unpleasant news. I was to be admitted to hospital where the doctors could monitor my condition. Now, I have had several interactions with hospitals and hospital personnel in various countries, and associated them with inconvenience, distress, painful jabs, bright lights and sleepless nights, and death. I dreaded hospitals! However, I realised that my options were limited. So, I was admitted to the female general ward, where my case was turned over to the supervising doctor of in-patient care, Dr. Kassim, who was also the general surgeon. He came to see me during the ward rounds the following morning.

"Good morning," he said, brightly. We were already well acquainted. I had taught both of his children in primary school. He inquired as to how I had slept, and whether there were any changes in the dripping from my nostril. I told him there was no change.

"We are expecting a team of neurosurgeons from the United States this weekend," he said, to my great surprise. It was Wednesday. The weekend was only three days away. "They will spend a few days here and I am going to ask them to see you."

I breathed deeply. This was completely unexpected, and a wave of hope swept over me.

"Until then," the doctor continued, "we are going to keep you in hospital so we can monitor your condition. We have to make sure that you do not get any infection, so we will give you some antibiotics to prevent any chance of that."

He turned to leave. "Try and limit your movements," he cautioned, "so that you can minimise the amount of fluid dripping from your nose."

About twenty-five years earlier, in New Jersey, USA, a twelve-year-old boy, the youngest of a close-knit family of Bahamian immigrants, was given the book *Gifted Hands* written by Dr. Ben Carson. Dr. Carson, a pioneering African American neurosurgeon, had overcome numerous obstacles to become, at the age of thirty-three, head of paediatric neurosurgery at the world-famous Johns Hopkins Hospital. On reading Dr. Carson's story, the young boy, already a football hopeful, was deeply inspired, particularly by the way Dr. Carson had successfully separated twins conjoined at the occipital lobe of the brain. An unshakeable determination to be a neurosurgeon himself became a personal goal.

With strong parental guidance, this young boy developed into a disciplined young man, combining athletics and academics with enviable excellence and precision. Bolstered by an active personal Christian faith, he overcame obstacles, won scholarships to prestigious schools (including a Rhodes scholarship to Oxford University), played professional American football, graduated from medical school, and pursued his childhood dream to become a neurosurgeon. By March 2022, he was a senior neurosurgery resident in one of the most advanced Neurosurgery programmes in the United States, at Harvard-Massachusetts General Hospital. His name is Dr. Myron L. Rolle.[6]

Dr. Rolle had always maintained a close connection with the Bahamas, his ancestral home, and the rest of the Caribbean would benefit from this connection. The untimely death of a close relative in one of the smaller islands of the Bahamas, due to the inaccessibility of prompt neurosurgical care at that time, motivated him to set up the Caribbean Neurosurgery Foundation (CNF).[7] This Foundation, established in 2021, aimed to build neurosurgical capacity within the Bahamas, and in the wider Caribbean by extension. In 2021, a CNF team of neurosurgical practitioners, including Dr. Rolle, visited a few Caribbean territories like Jamaica and Guyana. In 2022, the team planned to branch out further, and to visit Montserrat and Antigua in early April.

And so it was, just a few days after the onset of my medical condition, that three neurosurgeons arrived at my bedside at the Glendon Hospital in Montserrat. Dr. William Butler, Dr. Michael Groff, and Dr. Myron Rolle warmly greeted me and listened carefully as I recounted my 'runny nose' experience. During the focused dialogue and medical examination which followed, the doctors demonstrated a most reassuring level of empathy and knowledge about my condition. No doubt about it – help had arrived!

What were the chances that a team of skilled and experienced health professionals, in the exactly needed medical discipline, would arrive in the exactly required location at exactly the right time to handle my medical situation? This was nothing short of a miracle, and caused deep reflection on the numerous ways in which outstanding episodes of Divine Providence had occurred in my life.[8] Some of these very difficult situations were discovered, decades later, to have rebounded in huge advantages to my well-being, and my ability to serve God and my community in various (and most humbling) ways. These reflections, on how God has led my life through many unexpected paths, and of His faithfulness in steering me through it all, despite periods of rebellion, unfaithfulness, and sheer obstinacy, have given my faith a new dimension.

This was not the first time that I had found myself in a situation where I felt the heavy weight of uncertainty. But this time, from what I had found out in researching my runny nose, it appeared that my life was under threat, and in a location without resources ready at hand to remove the threat.

As I pondered this, my thoughts were drawn to the story, told in 1 Kings 17, of Elijah, the prophet of God, who was hiding for his life in a ravine at Cherith. There, he survived on the food which scavenger birds would bring daily, and on the water from the nearby brook. And then, the brook dried up. Water, that most critical element for life, was no longer available. But God was not taken by surprise. He had already prepared a way for His servant – in this case, the "way" was a widow in Zarephath – over eighty miles away. Although she was herself in need, her heart had been Divinely prepared to offer Elijah the life-saving sustenance he badly needed.

Admittedly, I am no Elijah, but it is awe-inspiring to see how, just like in Elijah's situation, our Father God had carefully prepared persons, circumstances, and opportunities unknown to me, to providentially intersect with my life with perfect timing, to make ways where there seemingly were no ways. When Psalm 27:14 (ESV) charges me to "*wait for the Lord; be strong, and let your heart take courage; wait for the Lord*", I have a deeper appreciation of the strength of this command. With renewed clarity, I have learned to trust God. I have learned the absolute reality of the promise which the prophet Jeremiah relayed to God's people in exile: "*For I know the plans I have for you, declares the LORD, plans for welfare and not for evil, to give you a future and a hope"* (Jeremiah 29:11 ESV).

These reflections have been written in the hope that readers will be encouraged likewise to trust God's unfailing hand of guidance, secure and confident in His sovereignty and foreknowledge. In times of heart-wrenching disappointment, hope and peace can be found in the assurance that He is in control, even when the present reality contradicts our faith. And even though our hopes and dreams may not have the exact outcomes we desired, time will eventually show us that God's plans were better.

Often, this realisation does not happen immediately, but comes to us as we look back over times in our lives when we faced challenges or found ourselves in tricky situations. And then we see how these challenges and situations had been resolved in unexpected or even miraculous ways. This is how it has been in my life, and I have been blessed to trace so many providential outcomes at every turn of my life, from the very beginning.

CHAPTER TWO

Beginnings

I wish I had known my father much better than I did. Apart from a few occasional brief visits to see us, and even more occasional letters, he was mostly absent from my life after I turned seven or eight, when he and my mother separated. When he passed away in August 1969, I had not seen him for almost five years. I was seventeen years old. His siblings, my paternal aunts and uncles, did all they could to fill the gap, and their efforts were, and still are, deeply appreciated. I am extremely fond of them and their children, my cousins. Because of them, I came to know much more about Daddy and his side of the family.

My father's bloodline stemmed from the union (reported to be unwilling) between black former enslaved women and their white British overseers, on nearby sugar plantations in

Jamaica, around the middle of the 19th century. The names of the enslaved women are not known, but the names of the British fathers are, since the resulting mulatto offspring took the surnames of their fathers.

Although chattel slavery had been abolished in Jamaica for at least fifteen years by then, those former slaves who continued to work on the plantations did so under a form of wage-slavery.[9] This was different from chattel slavery under which enslaved Africans on the plantations of the New World were considered to be property that could be bought and sold at will. They were forced to labour without compensation at the owners' behest, under terrible physical and psychological conditions. Wage-slavery existed because the former slave owners still owned or controlled most of the land and the means of production in the colonies. Thus, although the former slaves were now held to be legally emancipated, in order to survive, many of them had little option but to continue to work on the plantations under rules so strict and wages so low, that they were now effectively slaves of a different order.

Theresa Wilson was the mulatto daughter of a black wage-slave on the Walton sugar plantation in Hanover, Jamaica. On an adjoining plantation, another black wage-slave gave birth to a mulatto son whom she named Lewis Hylton. These mothers knew each other and arranged for their children Theresa and Lewis to marry. That union produced seven children. I was privileged to meet Theresa and Lewis' last child, my great-grand-aunt Constance, in 1967. She was, by then, very old and mostly bed-bound, and she passed away soon after.

My Dad, Frankie, was the great-grandson of Theresa and Lewis Hylton through his mother, Ena. I never knew my paternal grandparents, but learned that my grandfather, Robert Dewar, was a baker. My grandmother, Ena, was a seamstress, and had taught high school French for a short time until she became pregnant out of wedlock with my father, her first child, and thereby lost her job. Although she later married Robert Dewar, and together they produced six more children, Ena was ostracised by her family. She died of cancer when Frankie was fourteen, and her youngest, Ruby, was just eight months old. Ena had raised her children on the family property at Walton Estate, where her aunt Constance also lived. Family members adopted Ena's four middle children during the weeks following her death. But her two oldest (Frankie and Daphne) and her youngest (Ruby) remained with their grand-aunt Constance on the Walton Estate.

A bright young man, Frankie won a scholarship to the Jamaica School of Agriculture, and shortly after graduation he secured a job in another Caribbean island, Montserrat, as an Agricultural Officer. Some of the elders in Montserrat remember that he was assigned to handle the Ottway land development programme at Amersham, on the outskirts of the capital, Plymouth. They also remember him riding a motorcycle as his primary means of transportation, and some even recall that he rode so fast, he earned the nickname "Flying Blind." After his stint in Montserrat, Frankie returned to Jamaica. World War II was raging in Europe, and the British were recruiting personnel from their colonies to serve the war effort. Frankie joined the Royal Air Force in Jamaica, and was promptly shipped out to England.

My mother, Doreen Margetson, was born in St Kitts, the first child of the marriage between Dr. Noel Margetson (from St Kitts) and Clara Adelaide Steele, (who was born in St Ann's

Bay, Jamaica). My mother's subsequent marriage to Frankie Dewar seemed like another "coincidence," as in the case of both her parents and herself, both partners were a mix of Jamaicans and Kittitians, all of whom would come to have a connection with Montserrat.

My maternal grandparents met in New York City, where my grandmother's family had migrated when she was a child. My grandfather had gone there to study medicine. All my grandfather's siblings - his brothers Edward "Teddy" and Karl, and his younger sister Evelyn - had migrated to New York as young adults, and were all gifted professional pianists and piano teachers. My grandmother, Clara, was a contralto singer of considerable talent. I never heard how my grandparents met, but I like to think that music played a part in it, possibly through my grandfather's close relationship with his musical siblings.

After their marriage, my grandparents lived for a short time in St Kitts, where my mother was born in 1924. Then my grandfather accepted the position of Surgeon at the hospital in Montserrat, and in 1925, the family moved to Montserrat, where four other children (Noel Jr., Robert "Bobby", Gwendolyn, and Franklin) were born.

After leaving school, my mother, Doreen, boarded a ship bound for Britain to pursue a career in nursing. There she met Frankie Dewar. (I always assumed they met through mutual Montserratian friends whom Frankie knew from his period of residence in Montserrat.) By then, Doreen was a recently qualified Registered Nurse and Midwife. Frankie and Doreen were married in 1951, and I entered the world as their first child in London, on April 7, 1952.

Doreen became pregnant again a few months later. Knowing the challenges of earning an income while raising two children under the age of two, in an era of some hostility to persons of Afro-Caribbean descent, it was decided that she would travel to Antigua where her parents now resided. Her father, Dr. Noel Margetson had by then left Montserrat for Antigua to take up a position as Surgeon Specialist at the Holberton Hospital. So, at seven months pregnant, Doreen flew with ten-month-old Ann Marie to Antigua, where her second child, a daughter named Beverley Joy, was born on April 22,1953. Doreen subsequently was offered a nursing position on the neighbouring island of Nevis, and Frankie shortly thereafter followed her to Nevis, where he entered employment as an Agriculturist.

I do not remember much of my early years, especially of life in Nevis. I do not remember anything about schooling, or of early instruction. However, I do remember the joy of living with both parents under the same roof, and of a happy young childhood in Nevis. My main memory, though, is of having terrible pain in my lower right abdomen caused by appendicitis, and of undergoing the frightening experience of hospitalisation, emergency surgery, and recovering from the surgery at just five years old.

My idyllic nuclear family situation was noticeably spiralling into conflict, however, leading to the eventual separation of my parents (they never divorced). When I was six years old, Mummy took Beverley and me to Antigua where she was appointed as a senior nurse at the Holberton Hospital. Beverley and I moved in with our maternal grandparents, and Mummy moved into designated housing on the hospital compound. And so it was that Beverley and I were raised by our grandparents for the next six years.

I was very inquisitive about my family members. My mother had four siblings who lived in Britain and Jamaica. Although most of them appeared in my christening photos taken in London, I did not know any of them until I was at least nine years old, when, over the next three years or so, they made visits to Antigua, sometimes alone, sometimes with their spouses and/or children.

Uncles Noel, Bobby, and Franklin were fun-loving and easy to like. We met Uncle Noel first. He was an ophthalmologist who lived in Jamaica, and was fond of "treating" his nieces, so of course, he became our favourite uncle! He bought us our first camera, a tiny Kodak which he showed us how to use. At that time, digital cameras were decades in the future, and we were oblivious to the expense of purchasing film and having the photos developed at the local photographic shop in Antigua.

When Uncle Bobby came to visit from the UK, he brought his little son, Robert Jr, whom we called Robin, and it was love at first sight. Robin was the first cousin we had met at that time. Beverley and I loved playing with him, and we were so sad when the visit was over.

Auntie Gwen, my mother's only sister, was one of the most beautiful women I had ever seen. While our relationship with her never blossomed into closeness, as with our uncles, she was truly kind, and brought a more modern approach to our upbringing. For example, she introduced television and stereo records to the household. While our access was strictly controlled, these modern media devices broadened our knowledge of classical and Broadway music, and our visual and practical understanding of world events which previously were only communicated audibly via radio.

One of the blessings which Auntie Gwen brought into my life was her acceptance of her cousin Dorothy, born outside of wedlock to my grandfather's brother. She had been virtually ignored by the rest of the family but was lovingly embraced by Auntie Gwen. Dorothy had grown up, married, and had children of her own, and one of her daughters, Valerie, was also a pupil at the same high school in Antigua I attended. I found out that I was related to Valerie because of the providential intervention of my Auntie Gwen. Valerie was a senior pupil, so I timidly sought her out, and admired her intensely. Her warm and friendly personality, caring nature, and love for family have maintained that admiration, undiminished. Over the years, having met her siblings, I found that these traits were shared. We were family!

Within a few years of each other, Uncle Franklin and all my mother's other siblings (except Uncle Noel) returned with their families to live in Antigua, and a most loving bond was formed with their children, my cousins Judy, Lesley, Keva, Robin, Craig, Suzanne, Sharon, and Julian.

My father had five living siblings. (One of his sisters, my aunt Daphne, had died soon after marriage, leaving three young sons.) These aunts and uncles of mine all lived in Jamaica, and Daddy spoke lovingly of them. However, I never met any of them until I was fifteen years old, when I visited Jamaica to try to reconnect with Daddy. There I met some of the most wonderful people I could have ever wished to be family. After staying for a few days with my mother's brother,

Uncle Noel, who lived in Montego Bay, I travelled by train to Kingston to meet Daddy's sister, my Aunt Grace, her husband, Uncle Keith, and their two daughters Debra and Lisa. What a wonderful reception they gave me! During the week or so I spent with them, they took me to meet other relatives, and I soon found just as much love and joy on my father's side of the family as I knew on my mother's side.

Uncle Sydney and Uncle-in-law Keith were both kind and thoughtful. Uncle Keith ran a bookstore, and he would let me spend time at the store, which was such a treat, as I loved books and reading just as much as I enjoyed being around him. Uncle Sydney, whom I saw almost daily, would often take me out with him, and showed so much care that I did not know how much more happiness my heart could hold.

I met Daddy's youngest sister, Aunt Ruby, and over the decades since then, both Aunts Grace and Ruby have continued to envelop me in love and caring support. Aunt Ruby's husband, Uncle Fred, and their children Audrey, Christopher, and Robert, treated me with equally outstanding kindness. I also came to know Michael, one of Aunt Daphne's sons, (whom we called Tony). Many years later, when I sojourned in London for a few years, I met Michael's brothers, my cousins Paul and Byford. Later, I also met Daddy's brothers Uncle Kenneth and Uncle William. I marvelled at how alike the Dewar men were in looks. It was uncanny!

Over the decades, I have met a few more cousins and family members on my father's side, including Carla (who lives in New York and showed Beverley and me amazing hospitality when we visited) and Uncle William's daughter, Grace (like me, also a career educator). In more recent times, social media opened the door to virtually meeting other cousins and has made it easier to stay in touch with those I've personally met. I treasure every contact and am blessed by each one.

But God was not done wrapping my life with supportive family, and as a young adult I was to find even more instances of providential planning. My mother's brother, Bobby, had married a Trinidadian nurse, Rose Brown, who was a colleague and friend of my mother's in England, where they trained together. My sister Beverley and I were closest in age to their children, and our friendship was so strong we called each other "sister-cousin" or "brother-cousin."

It was no surprise, then, that we grew close to their relatives on Aunt Rose's Trinidadian side of the family. We met all their aunts and uncles, and most of their cousins. Years later, when Beverley was diagnosed with breast cancer, it was to Trinidad that she went for her early treatments, and our Trinidadian family hosted her with immense kindness. When two of my work postings required attendance at annual meetings in Trinidad, they welcomed me with open arms. A few years later, when I needed orthopaedic treatment, they assisted in making the arrangements, and showed me the greatest hospitality. They would introduce me to their friends as a family member.

"Meet my cousin from Montserrat," they would say. Or "Come, I want you to meet my niece from Montserrat."

On one occasion in Trinidad, when I was out with my "Auntie" Katie, one of her friends tried to make sense of the relationship, and asked, "So Katie, how is she your niece?"

Neither Auntie Katie nor I was expecting that question. As far as we were concerned, we were just family, although not actual blood-relatives. But the friend quickly followed her question with another. "Is she Rose's daughter?"

Well, Aunt Rose was indeed regarded by both Beverley and me as our "second mother". We had grown up around her, and her home was our home whenever we travelled to Antigua. Her children were our closest cousins. After our mother died, Aunt Rose had come to stay with Beverley and me in Montserrat for a short while to help us through the initial grieving process. What we would have done without that loving intervention, I do not know. God had it all worked out!

"Yes," Auntie Katy responded firmly, "Rose's daughter."

I instantly had a most significant recollection. A few years before, Aunt Rose had sent me a birthday card. In it, she had written, "To my fourth daughter, Ann Marie, with love from Aunt Rose." Yes, I indicated by nodding my head. I was, indeed, "Rose's daughter." Trinidad soon became another home away from home.

The legendary South African cleric, Desmond Tutu, once made the profound statement that "...You don't choose your family. They are God's gift to you, as you are to them."[10] I have been increasingly grateful to God for providentially locating me within such a caring "village" of individuals whom I am privileged to call my family. I have known too many people whose experiences were far different from mine, who craved the kind of affection that I have known from family members, particularly in my adolescence and continuing into adulthood.

My extended family has been one of the pillars which have bolstered me from my earliest childhood, right through to the present time. How blessed I am to know these lovely individuals who make up my family network, and whose support and love continue to hold me accountable for my intentions, while adding much happiness (and, yes, lots of fun) every day.

CHAPTER THREE

Falling into Good Company

My friends, colleagues, mentees, and even some close family members have a tough time believing that I struggled with feelings of social and intellectual inferiority and inadequacy for most of my life. Psychologists may attribute some of this, in part, to a sense of isolation in my early childhood years. My sister and I were schooled privately until I was around eight. At that time, we only left the house in the company of one of our maternal grandparents, to go to Miss Pilgrim's private school (where Beverley and I were the only pupils), or to church with my grandfather, or to visit one of my grandparents' friends. My mother had been seconded from her senior nursing post at the Holberton hospital in Antigua to serve as Acting Matron at the hospital in Montserrat. She moved to Montserrat when I was seven years old, leaving Beverley and me in the care of our grandparents in Antigua. They, and their middle-aged friends, and our domestic helper, the deeply beloved Miss Eileen, were the only persons of close acquaintance.

It was different during the school holidays when we travelled to Montserrat to spend our vacations with our mother. Mummy was an extremely outgoing, sociable person, and she encouraged us to be the same. So we looked forward to going to Montserrat, and I am sure that our elderly grandparents welcomed the respite from their two young granddaughters as well. If school closed today, we would be in Montserrat tomorrow. If school re-opened tomorrow, we would be travelling back to Antigua today. Most of my friends during my primary school days were the friends we enjoyed during the holidays in Montserrat. But once back under our grandparents' roof, Beverley and I had only each other's company.

Beverley and I did find ways to occupy ourselves, and those were not always well thought out. One Sunday afternoon, for instance, we decided to play a game of rounders. We had no bat or ball. Our grandparents were taking a nap, so we quietly slipped outside and found a great spot on the large expanse of land away from the house. We scouted around and found an empty glass bottle lying in the grass, and nearby, there was a nice round stone. Bev was the bowler, and bowled the stone, while I held the glass bottle to bat it away. I swung, and the bottle expertly connected with the stone and shattered, sending a shard of broken glass straight into the middle of my forehead. Blood flowed instantly, and I ran screaming toward the house, with Beverley following closely behind. My grandfather went into surgeon mode, and patched me up in his surgery, before sharply scolding both of us. Divine Providence had prevented more serious damage to my head, given the speed and trajectory of the broken glass, and the incredible stupidity of our actions. Sixty years later, the scar is still there to remind me.

When our grandparents decided to send Beverley and me to an established school, we were enrolled at the Antigua Girls' High School. The school had a preparatory wing, and I was placed in Year Four. I was so excited about the opportunity to be with children of my age for several hours each day, but apprehensive as well since I was not used to being with other children in a formal school environment. I soon found that most of the other pupils already had their circle of friends, and I struggled with feelings of isolation, yearning to make friends and be accepted.

By this time, Beverley and I had been allowed to go by ourselves to Sunday School on Sunday afternoons at the Moravian church. My grandfather was partial to the Moravian church, as he had been raised Moravian as a youngster in St Kitts. The superintendent of the Moravian Sunday School was an acquaintance of theirs and had extended an invitation for Beverley and me to attend. We were, therefore, sent to Sunday school, and placed in the class of Miss Gloria Gordon, whom we immediately adored. Her Bible stories were lively, and she was young and extremely beautiful. We looked forward to attending. However, we did not make many friends there, since we were engaged in singing and active listening for the entire hour, and then we were picked up immediately afterwards and driven back home.

I did not fit in at school, as I did not do the things that trendy young people did. For one thing, my grandmother (whom we called Nanny) took her delegated responsibility for raising her first grandchildren (Beverley and me) very seriously, and that included ensuring that we were always appropriately dressed. I wanted to wear more fashionable clothes (Nanny sewed all our clothes). I wanted stylish shoes to wear to school, instead of plain lace-ups (boy's shoes, I called them). I wanted nice church shoes with a little heel, and I wanted to wear them without socks, as the trendy friends I desired were doing.

I wanted to go to the church bazaars (I could go to the Anglican one, but never to the Roman Catholic one) and to have a little more money to spend there (we got two dollars each to spend at the Anglican bazaar, while the popular friends we desired usually had at least five dollars or more). We never had pocket money, but once or twice a year, Nanny would take us to the small bookstore in town and let us buy an approved book.

The carnival season in Antigua was one of the most highly anticipated events each year. Judging by the classroom chatter, most of my classmates were going to participate in some of the festivities. I longed to attend the carnival too, especially the jump up on Carnival Monday and Tuesday, which were some of the highlights of the season, but I got the same negative answer every time I asked.

I knew better than to ask Nanny to allow me to hang out with classmates in town at the end of our weekly after-school sports sessions, but even when I took a chance and did so without permission, I felt like a tag-along since I was not socially a part of the group.

Eventually, to cultivate friendships with the popular crowd I resorted to activities that could have landed me in serious trouble. One of the milder instances occurred on an impulse one afternoon when I left home to go to piano lessons. I skipped the class and went to spend time with a popular girl who had been friendly and kind to me. We sat outside her home and chatted freely. I felt I had a friend, although she was several years older than I. When I returned home, Nanny asked me where I had been, and as soon as I uttered the words "to music," I knew that she knew I had been delinquent. Of course, the music teacher had called to enquire about me since I had not turned up for class. Nanny was drinking some water when I arrived home. When I told an obvious lie, she doused me with the remaining water, and while I tried to clear the water from my eyes, she gave me a sound thrashing. I apologised for the two sins of commission and omission and did not try that again. However, that did not stop the deep yearning for friendships and acceptance, especially among my peers at school.

I admired other young people who appeared strong, were accomplished, and had achieved success in academics or athletics, or any other area. I marvelled at the musical skill of one older student, Margaret Armstrong, who played the piano exquisitely, and was called upon often to accompany the hymns we sang at school assemblies. When she asked me to help with page-turning, I was star-struck, and more than happy to oblige. I think I did the job well, as she asked me often. I wanted to be able to play hymns and accompany singing just like she did. She inspired me. I was also highly motivated by other students who seemed very self-assured, and one of these was my older cousin, Valerie. She was beautiful, popular, and seemed very wise. I sought her out during school recess breaks and was thrilled when she did not push me away but allowed me to stay with her even while she conversed with her peer group.

However, there were some students and teachers who did not think that lower school students should hang around with more senior students. I remember one incident with a teacher for whom I had huge respect. I'll refer to her as Miss Clarke. She was our Latin teacher. I liked Latin a lot and found Miss Clarke to be a great teacher. She was strict, but pleasant, and I did well in her class. One day when I was in the Second Form, I was standing outside the Fifth Form classroom waiting to speak to a senior girl. Miss Clarke came along and asked me what I was doing there. I explained that I was waiting for a senior student. A look of sheer disgust appeared on her face.

"Go away," she commanded in a most unpleasant tone, a nasty grimace on her face. "The sight of you makes my flesh creep!"

I was mortified and felt physically sick. I ran away as fast as I could, still not believing what had been said to me by one of my favourite teachers. A pall descended over me. It occurred to me that even a teacher whom I respected so highly, did not like me. In fact, she loathed me if just seeing me could generate that much disgust. I had never had any reason to suspect this. I was deeply distressed. I was heartbroken. If she felt that way, did other teachers or even my schoolmates think the same of me?

My grandmother sensed my distress and asked me what was wrong. I told her what Miss Clarke had said to me. She was horrified but was not one to accost a teacher. I believe she may have expressed some displeasure to the headmistress, but I heard nothing about this from anyone at the school. Miss Clarke certainly never mentioned anything further about it.

Not that I expected an apology. However, my grandmother told my mother about the incident. Mummy lived and worked in Montserrat at that time. She was livid, and I believe that if she could, she would have travelled to Antigua to the school and accosted Miss Clarke as well as the headmistress. However, she reassured me of her love, and I felt truly supported by her in this incident. Many years later, she recalled the matter, and expressed to me how angry she was that a teacher could have said such a thing to a child.

But even when the darkness of loneliness, alienation, and despair threatened to overwhelm, God found a way to lighten the darkness. In my pre-teen years, this may not have been understood or obvious. However, in hindsight and with the experience of adulthood, clarity appeared. There was one classmate whom I first met in Year Four and who gradually became a light in my darkness. Her name was Cecile Wood, and we called her Elinor. I do not remember how we became friends, but I could not have wished for a more wonderful friend and role model. I do not recall ever visiting Elinor's home, or meeting her family, but she was such an outstanding person in her own right. We were opposites in many ways. She was a strong, self-motivated person. I could not have been more different. But she demonstrated friendship consistently, and I treasured that friendship with every ounce of my being.

I recall a class competition in making the best doll's dress. We were about nine years old, and both Elinor and I were entering the competition. We both desperately wanted to win. Her doll's dress easily won, and I was so happy for her that I did not even sulk about not winning. Her friendship prevented me from dropping to the bottom of the barrel in my quest for popularity and belonging. Over the next three years or so, as I fought pre-adolescent angst, I now had a friend to whom I could relate, whom I saw every school day. Her stabilising influence helped to bolster my self-confidence, and calm the churning storm of loneliness and feelings of inferiority which at times threatened to engulf me.

My grandmother, however, had had quite enough of my incorrigible attitude and behaviour. With more than a generational gap between us, I imagine it was difficult for her to deal with the responsibility and accountability of raising a self-centred pre-teen girl. She tried her absolute best and was a wonderful grandmother. Both Beverley and I learned so much about refinement from her.

Nanny and Grandad were a real-life finishing school. We learned how to set a table properly, how to correctly use a variety of knives and forks, how to 'eat' soup, how to curtsy, how to address older persons, how to make a variety of canapés and desserts, how to make proper English breakfasts, and how to darn, mend, sew, and iron our own clothes. We learned how to thinly peel vegetables with a knife so that we retained nutrients, how to properly turn pages in a book and how to cover books. We learned how to write and address letters, and how to disappear appropriately when adult company came to visit.

Beverley and I also had some of our first lessons on the importance of service from our grandparents. Service to God and to the community was just part of the culture at our home in Antigua, where commitment demanded setting priorities. When our eagerly anticipated Monday afternoon dance classes clashed with the scheduled after-school sports sessions for my new year group at high school, my grandfather made me give up dance classes. I was a member of the school body, he insisted, and therefore the programme of the school had to have my primary commitment. I was heartbroken, but Grandad was firm. So, while Beverley went to dance classes, I went to the sports sessions at school. But I learned the lesson well and have carried it with me throughout my life.

It had been decided that Beverley and I would complete my Third Form (and Beverley's Second Form) high school year in Antigua, and then move permanently to Montserrat to begin school there from September 1964. However, in late July 1964, Grandad became ill, and was admitted to hospital. Beverley and I were on school holidays, and normally, we would have already gone to Montserrat for the summer vacation. But since we were moving permanently for the new school year, it was agreed that we would spend some of the summer in Antigua with Nanny and Grandad, and then move to Montserrat at the end of August.

It was now the beginning of August, carnival time in Antigua. I badly wanted to go to town to watch the festivities, especially the jump-up on Carnival Monday. Nanny had been spending a lot of time at the hospital with Grandad, and I needed to seek her permission. I knew she totally disapproved of our attending carnival activities except when we could be escorted to the children's carnival. But I was determined to go and decided that I would call her at the hospital and ask her permission. So, on Carnival Monday morning, I called the hospital and spoke to her. She sounded weary, exhausted, like the fight had gone out of her. I heard it in her voice. But still, I asked her if I could go to the carnival in town. I will never forget her words, softly spoken, in a monotone of resignation. She drew a tired breath.

"Do whatever you like, Ann Marie," she said.

I was elated for a moment. I had asked and had not been denied. I thought about what I would wear. The way was clear for me to escape the house, and get away for some excitement, with permission to do so. This was an unusual situation, one which felt too good to be true. But as I thought about it more, I realised that I had not really been given permission. The ball had been thrown, wearily, into my court. The decision was mine to make. Should I go, or should I not go? What questions would I be asked once Nanny got home? Suppose something happened to me while I was in town.

The thought settled on me that I should not go. It was a jarring thought since I really wanted to go to the carnival. I was conflicted. But in the end, I did not go. I did not know then, that while I was mentally debating whether to go to the carnival or not, Grandad was drawing his last breaths in the hospital, with Nanny, his wife of forty-two years, at his bedside.

Nanny came home very early the next morning in a sombre mood. She told us that Grandad had died. Beverley and I were speechless. Grandad was a monumental part of our lives and had been since we were old enough to know who he was. We did not realise that he was so sick, and at the point of dying. A vacuum threatened to suck me in. I was numb, bewildered, and frightened. Neither Beverley nor I had ever experienced death up close before.

I felt incredibly guilty for having called Nanny the morning before to ask if I could do something as silly as go to the carnival jump-up. I had been oblivious to other concerns. What had seemed so urgent and necessary then now appeared so stupid, so self-centred, so uncaring. I never forgot that experience. Nanny never scolded me or told me how insensitive

I had been. I suspect she was just too heartbroken and numb herself to do so. But there was One who helped me to unravel my thoughts, recognise my own self-centredness, and quietly led me into serious introspection over the incident, although it did not happen immediately.

Mummy travelled to Antigua within a few hours of Grandad's death. As usual in those days, funeral arrangements were quickly made. Grandad's funeral was a massive one. As a gifted medical practitioner and surgeon, he was well known. It was the final day of carnival, with the usual last-lap jump up, but many people turned their backs on the carnival and came out to pay their last respects to Grandad.

After the funeral, family members gathered at the family home on Fort Road. Nanny was speaking to Mummy in a separate room, away from the rest of the family. I came into the room. Nanny looked at me, and then at Mummy.

"Doreen," Nanny said to Mummy, "when you return to Montserrat, take Ann Marie with you. Beverley can stay a little longer."

Nanny looked at me again, and I knew. She was exhausted from trying. She had had enough. Losing Grandad was soul-numbing. She had no energy left to engage my stubbornness. She was done. And so was any discussion on the matter.

Mummy was returning to Montserrat in two days' time, and those days were spent in packing, and in a whirlwind of mental activity. I was excited to be going to Montserrat with Mummy, but I was bewildered at the thought of Beverley not being with me. We had never been apart since she was born. And I was still filled with guilt that my bad attitude and behaviour had got Nanny so fed up with me that she was "throwing me out" by not allowing me to stay with Beverley until the time agreed for us to move to Montserrat.

I wish I could say that moving to Montserrat and living with my mother initiated an immediate and positive change in my attitude and conduct. It did not. I still craved popularity and wanted to be a part of the trendy set. In my mind, those were the ones who got noticed, who were admired (at least by me), and who exuded confidence and influence. But my twelve-going-on-thirteen-year-old mind did not readily grasp the dangers of rushing in where angels fear to tread, and impulsive behaviour was often employed as the means to gaining attention. It took a literally painful episode to make me see the folly of this.

One of the teachers at school was a wonderful role model, an incredibly talented musical artist, and a very disciplined and cultured woman. A no-nonsense person, she held herself to high standards, and expected the same of all her students. We knew this. So why did I think that I could be downright disrespectful to her and get away with it?

It was the last day of my first academic year at school in Montserrat. I was chatting in a group with some other students, including my sister Beverley. A boy in my class interrupted our conversation to convey a message that this teacher wished to see me. Without engaging my mental faculties which would have cautioned me that my immediate thought was stupid, irrational, insubordinate, and completely unwarranted, I blurted out a response. I used an abominably coarse and unrepeatable phrase, and told the boy to tell the teacher what I said. It was said so matter-of-factly that there was mild mirth from the other students, and we continued our conversation. No one really expected the boy to convey my message. I fully intended to go to see the teacher, but, of course, could not appear to be rushing to obey a command, and wanted to get my little moment of badness in before I trekked up to the staff room.

I never got that far. Within minutes, I received a peremptory summons to the headmaster's office, and of course, that did not allow for any hesitancy on my part. The headmaster, who was also a close family friend (and whom my sister and I called Uncle outside of school), got straight to the point, and asked me to relate the message which I had sent to the teacher. I was stunned. I was cornered. I tried every way I could think of to make it seem less than it was. I beat around the bush. The male messenger had, alas, already relayed the names of witnesses to my obscene message, and of them all, the headmaster sent to call my sister. He pointedly asked Beverley what I had said, and my darling sister related it word-for-word.

I got a sound scolding from the headmaster, but that was not all. I was sentenced to a "report", which carried with it a form of corporal punishment that has now, happily, been banned from schools in Montserrat. The punishment was delivered in private. Since I was a female, the headmaster left the office, a designated female teacher entered, and the doors were shut. But it was not a private thing at all since the sounds of a whip striking one's back could be heard through the closed doors, and news of a "report" spread like wildfire through the school.

The female teacher did not shirk in carrying out her duty. The first lash was excruciating. The other eleven strokes piled on top of the first were indescribably painful. But it was neither the punishment with its attending pain and humiliation, nor the lingering physical soreness that jolted me into an overpowering sense of shame at my display of outrageous attitude and behaviour. It was the look of profound disappointment on my mother's face and in her eyes, when she was summoned to the school by the headmaster, and told of her daughter's defiance, and coarse, disrespectful utterance.

I was immediately suspended, which was of little effect since it was the last day of school before the summer holidays. On the drive home, Mummy quietly expressed her deep disappointment, and cautioned me never to repeat that behaviour. She did not shout at me; she did not spank me (I do not recall ever being spanked by Mummy – a look from her was usually sufficient). There was no further discussion about the matter. Mummy expected that one word of caution was enough. Beverley and I both loved her deeply, and appreciated the sacrifices and the unrelenting effort she made in ensuring that we were well taken care of and learned good values. I was determined never to let her down like this again.

Mummy was not alone in raising us. Providentially, we had an entire "village" who were all invested in our success, although we only realised the extent of it as we grew into adulthood. My mother was matron of the only hospital in Montserrat, and until her retirement when we were late teens, we lived in the "Matron's House" at the edge of the hospital compound. So, we were surrounded by a close-knit team of hospital workers – maids, laundry staff, ambulance drivers, orderlies, nurses, and even some administrative staff, who all took on various roles as carers, mentors, advisers, counsellors, and stern guardians to "Matron Dewar's daughters" as, and when, they felt it was needed. Most of these elders had families of their own, and some had only the most basic education. Through God's grace, they took upon themselves the additional charge of correcting, encouraging, and nurturing Beverley and me into becoming the best young ladies we could be. This continued right up to adulthood.

My mother embraced the "village". Later on, she recounted to us several incidences of being approached by one or more of the hospital staff to admonish her about the type of persons we were seen in company with, or behaviours they had observed. There was even one person who suggested that my mother get us some "birth control pills" as she thought we had boyfriends. Mummy did actually ask us about this, and we truthfully told her that the only pill we needed was aspirin when we got a headache.

Mummy was well liked in the community. She was a good cook, and I remember instances when persons in the community would arrive at our doorstep with skinned iguanas and ask her to cook them. And she did. The same folks would return a few hours later with gratitude to take away their well-seasoned, tender, and tasty delicacy. Neither Beverley nor I ever volunteered to do the taste test. The sight of large, skinned iguanas was too much for our stomachs to overcome.

Our friends were welcomed to our home. The only stipulations I remember were that they had to leave by 8.30p.m., and sound levels had to be strictly contained so as not to disturb the patients and staff at the hospital, which was mere yards away from the house. Mummy set the example. She was an avid jazz music fan and had a huge collection of albums – Dizzy Gillespie, The Dave Brubeck Quartet, Louis

Armstrong, Ella Fitzgerald; name the popular jazz musicians of the day and it was very likely that she had at least one of their albums. Radio DJs used to borrow from her collection.

After work and on weekends, there was jazz on the record player, but it was turned down low, producing sweet background melodies while she cooked or did other household chores, or relaxed. In Mummy's mind, when we sat down to dinner, or friends dropped by, we needed to be able to converse quietly, but easily, with the soft background music creating an aura of calmness, enabling greater enjoyment of food and friends.

When Mummy spoke, she did so softly. I cannot recall her raising her voice, even when she was upset. In fact, it seemed to us that the more upset she was, the more she lowered her voice. These may be the reasons why to this day, I cannot tolerate loud music or inordinate shouting. I learned early on the benefits of quiet environments in which to meditate, worship, study, converse, and relax. This set me on course to develop keen listening skills, including predicting and responding to subtle nuances in music. Over time, it also helped me to develop skills in choral and instrumental music arranging and harmonisation, and honed my ability to play the piano by ear.

Like many other parents of my day, Mummy viewed reading as a critical skill for her children, and she sought to cultivate this habit in Beverley and me. Out of her limited means, she bought a set of encyclopaedias which I devoured, one at a time. I read each book as if it were a novel. I read everything, every entry. In the volume labelled "L" I came across an article about a Swedish singer named Jenny Lind whom I had never heard of before, but now learned that she had such a beautiful voice she was nicknamed "the Swedish Nightingale." Such seemingly 'useless' pieces of information somehow stayed with me as I read the entries over and over.

Years later, Radio Antilles, a local radio station with Caribbean-wide coverage, hosted a quiz between local teams. I was invited to compete on one of the teams, and I remember one round, with the following trivia question: "Who was called the Swedish Nightingale?" It seemed such an irrelevant question for a competition based in the tiny Caribbean island of Montserrat. Here, the music and singers were more likely to be aligned with calypso, reggae, and US or British-based pop songs, rather than those of Europe or, in this case, Scandinavia. Team members competing in that round raised their eyebrows and gave looks suggesting they had not even heard of the "Swedish Nightingale," much less to name her. But I raised my hand boldly.

"Jenny Lind," I answered. I still remember the looks of astonishment from both teammates and competitors.

This was a small friendly competition for entertainment purposes, and neither I nor my team won fortune or fame because of it. However, the incident helped me to realise that Mummy's investment had paved the way for me to contribute to my team. It underscored for me the importance of reading, gaining knowledge, and of being willing to share that knowledge when needed. The important thing was to utilise opportunities to improve myself consistently, and those improvements would rebound to benefit myself and others in the longer term. A small, but illustrative example of the ways in which opportunities (i.e., access to encyclopaedias) placed in my life by a caring mother, prepared me for an unrelated event several years in the future, both circumstance and event intersecting in an unplanned and unforeseen way.

As I reflected on this, I was able to draw parallels with the ways in which Divine Providence had led me through the winding course of my life, directing each turn, including those of my childhood and teenage years. This included growing up as an adolescent in Montserrat, in an environment of firm mentors and trusted friendships. The strong community and service-oriented perspective which informed my mother's worldview, and the specific ground rules and high expectations for my behaviour, were undoubtedly by providential design. I indeed "fell" into good company and was nurtured in an environment in which I learned the value of respect, tranquillity, self-discipline, loving correction, and accountability not only to myself, family, and school, but also to the community at large.

I learned to think of others, and not just of myself. Had this shift not occurred, who knows how the trajectory of my life might have unfolded.

CHAPTER FOUR

Developing Faith

God in His providence allowed us to be raised by our grandparents in our most formative years. While I do not remember my grandmother attending church regularly, my grandfather was an ardent churchgoer, especially on Sunday mornings. Beverley and I were given no choice in going to church with him.

Grandad had been raised in the Moravian church. However, when he moved to Montserrat to work as a medical doctor and surgeon, he found no Moravian churches on the island. Thus, he joined the Anglican church. When he left Montserrat and moved to Antigua some twenty-two years later, he continued to faithfully attend the Anglican church there, and when Beverley and I came along, he took us in tow. I developed an interest in the Christian faith at an early age. We were enrolled in the Moravian Sunday school, where the marvellous teacher named Gloria Gordon inspired me even at that early age. Sitting in her Sunday school classes, concepts of faith and Christian values were firmly inculcated, with strong doses of Bible stories as evidence.

Neither of my parents were professing Christians beyond a nominal faith. I have no memories of my mother ever attending church except for christenings, weddings, and funerals. When I was older, I remember asking her why she did not attend church, and she related a story of being offended by a comment from an Anglican minister years earlier, and she just never went back to Sunday services.

After Beverley and I moved permanently to Montserrat, we continued the tradition set by our grandfather, and we regularly attended Sunday morning services at the St Anthony's Anglican church. Mummy drove us to church, and we walked home unless some kind parishioner offered to give us a lift. As a teenager, I yearned in my spirit to understand faith and God. I felt a pull to deeper spirituality but did not fully understand what that was or how to go about it. This tug also led me to attend Lenten evening services, and I loved the gospel hymns in the *Mirfield Mission* hymn book from which we sang at these services.

Sometime after I entered the Montserrat Secondary School, an invitation was extended to join the Inter-School Christian Fellowship (ISCF), an after-school club which met on Thursday afternoons. I was surprised at the considerable number of students who were present at those meetings, which I found to be well organised, interactive, and extremely interesting. After a brief time of singing gospel songs and choruses, the meetings consisted of one or two different activities such as Bible studies, guest speakers, prayer time, Bible quizzes, or short prepared presentations by students on topics as varied as the stories behind well-known hymns, or lessons from the lives of Bible characters.

I thoroughly enjoyed the meetings and was a loyal attendee. Most importantly, I heard the gospel. I learned and understood, for the first time, that being a Christian was much more than attending church. Much more than reading a few scriptures, singing hymns, and saying prayers. I was really understanding, for the first time, that it was about believing that God had sent His only Son, Jesus, into the world to live a sinless life on behalf of sinful humans; that He bore the punishment for our sins on the cross; that He suffered and died, the just for the unjust, and that those who truly believed in His atoning work might have righteousness imputed to them by a just God.

My understanding is clearer now, several decades later, but at that time, my fourteen-year-old mind was slowly being opened, and I was both thrilled and moved by what I was learning at these ISCF meetings. I still attended the Anglican church but was also finding a "church" within the ISCF meetings at school.

It was in ISCF that God brought a special group of young people into my life, who from that point onwards intersected with my life in a most outstanding way. Over time, I found myself being drawn to friendship with this group of young people, especially the siblings Lazelle, Blondina, Orwyn, and Oral Howes, whose father was the pastor of the Bethany Pentecostal church in Plymouth.

There was another occurrence which initiated my entrance to a further dimension in what was beginning to be my walk with Christ. As a carry-over from my schooling in Antigua, I loved Latin, despite the betrayal of the teacher there. So, I was delighted to find that Latin was offered as a subject at the Montserrat Secondary School. The class was taught by an outstanding teacher who also happened to be a professing Christian. His name was Howard Fergus. As it turned out, he attended the same church (Bethany Pentecostal) as the Howes family and was a leader of the youth group at the church. One day, Mr. Fergus extended an invitation to me to attend Youth Week at the Bethany Pentecostal church. The youth group, which went by the name *Christ's Ambassadors*, was going to be having special services each night for the next week, led by the young people themselves.

I was extremely interested and excited to attend the Youth Week meetings, to which I knew several of my friends from ISCF would be going. But there was one drawback. I had to obtain permission from my mother, who had a very decided disdain for these small 'mission' type evangelical church denominations. I knew this, because of the comments she dropped from time to time when we passed these churches while services were going on.

There was one such church on the corner of the road leading to the home of friends whom we visited from time to time. On Friday evenings, there was a prayer meeting, and the church folks would kneel with their elbows resting on the seats of the pews. In that position, they would be facing the back of the church, away from the front or altar of the church. To an Anglican, even a nominal one, the altar of the church is the most sacred section of the church, where the priest presides over the blessing and serving of the Eucharist. It did not matter that the rituals of the 'mission' churches were quite different. As far as Mummy was concerned, these people were praying “with their backsides to the altar”.

The clapping to rhythmic music, singing and shouting were further strikes against these ‘wayside’ churches. Their joyful expression of praise, like the posture of prayer, appeared to Mummy to be irreverent. Nevertheless, my eagerness to accept the invitation to fellowship with the youth during Youth Week was so strong that I found the courage to ask her permission to attend. And against all my fears, she said yes. I was allowed to attend! Knowing how she felt about these churches and knowing that she had no qualms about saying no when she was not comfortable with our requests, I am convinced that a loving Heavenly Father, in His providence, moved on her heart and secured her permission.

The evenings spent at the Bethany Pentecostal Church’s Youth Week services changed my outlook on life in a positive way. Not only was I spiritually energised by the worship, the stirring meetings, the friendliness of the church folk, and the warmth of their welcome. I felt at home there. I wanted to learn more, to worship more. I wanted to know God for myself. And, despite my obvious unworthiness, I just wanted God to know me.

After the overwhelming experience of Youth Week, and in my deep desire to know God more, I continued to attend the Bethany Pentecostal church, but with some displeasure from Mummy. I did not wish to annoy her with continual requests to go to church, but there was a yearning within me which I could not deny. I was almost fifteen by then. Some of my school friends attended the Pentecostal church and lived a short distance from both my home and the church. Their mother was a devout believer, and always had words of encouragement for me. I passed their house on my way to town, school, and church. So, I would ask Mummy to go to their house, and she always said yes. I would go to visit my friends, and then run down to the church for about half an hour, and return to their home. They understood my deep desire to know and worship God. Then I would say goodbye and hurry home.

I did this from time to time on Sunday nights and sometimes during the week as well. There was a Testimony meeting on Monday nights, where old and young stood and spoke about the goodness of God in their lives and of incidents and episodes where God had shown favour or blessings. These were times of great motivation and encouragement in my faith. Tuesday nights were the best – youth meetings. To say they were exciting was an understatement. Some of my friends from ISCF led these thoroughly interesting and inspiring meetings. Friday was prayer meeting night. Although I could only stay for about half an hour at these services, it was a half-hour of joy, learning, increasing my faith, and growing in my understanding of the Christian journey.

In the meantime, ISCF meetings at school provided the support I needed to help me understand more about the Christian life. In early 1967, it was announced that there was to be an ISCF camp at Victory Heights in Trinidad. We were invited to consider attending, and to submit applications for the camp. I wanted to attend and was overwhelmed with joy when Mummy agreed that I could go. She sacrificed limited funds to enable my participation, and my camp registration was submitted. The ISCF in Trinidad connected me with a Christian family whose daughter was also attending the camp.

I stayed with this family on arrival in Trinidad and after camp, until my departure from Trinidad.

The ISCF camp was an amazing experience. There was wonderful camaraderie among the campers, almost all of whom were from various areas of Trinidad, and many were meeting each other for the first time, so I did not feel like an outsider. These young people were desirous of growing into a relationship with Christ. There were meaningful devotional times, exposition from the Word in simple terms to aid our understanding, and hugely enjoyable, fun-filled activities in the evenings. It became clear to me that I needed to cement the faith I had already been given by God's grace. I made a commitment to follow Christ. I was saved at that camp.

Returning home, I was on fire. I wanted to grow, to learn more, to solidify my faith. I sought to attend church as much as possible. Mummy was still not entirely happy with my attending the Pentecostal church, but I tried, with God's grace, to demonstrate a consistent Christian life at home. Eventually, she understood that my changed life was not a nine-day wonder, and it became easier for me to attend church on Sunday mornings and at reasonable times on weeknights, as long as my schoolwork did not suffer. She started calling me Sister Annie.

One Sunday morning, I did not attend church. I cannot now recall the reason for this, but Mummy came to my bedroom to inquire.

"Sister Annie," she said, "Aren't you going to church this morning?" I look back now and realise that this was a milestone moment. Mummy had finally accepted my desire to commit to a life of faith, which included church attendance to support my growth into that life of faith.

While Mummy had come to terms with my church preference, some of her friends had not. One afternoon after school, I went into a store in town to purchase an item. The owner of the store was a family friend, a well-known member of the elite social class on the island. He drew me aside in the store and berated me sternly as he had heard that I had joined that 'mission' church, which he felt was unbefitting of me. He let me know of his certainty that my fervour would not last. "I give you six months," he said.

I continued to attend ISCF meetings and church services and grew both in faith and fervour. Sometime after this, I followed the Lord in water baptism at Foxes Bay beach. I was the only candidate on that occasion, and two wonderful Pentecostal ministers briefly spoke to me and questioned me about my faith in Christ. They led me into the water and baptised me by full immersion. The following Sunday morning, I was received into fellowship in the Bethany Pentecostal church at Wapping in Plymouth, Montserrat.

This seed of faith, that had been providentially planted by my grandfather's example of devoted church attendance and Gloria Gordon's Sunday School classes in Antigua, was sprouting. It had been stirred by the Lenten services and gospel hymn singing at the St Anthony's Anglican Church. The ISCF watered it at the Montserrat Secondary School. The witness of Mr. Howard Fergus, my Latin and History teacher gave it the inspiration it needed, and the services at the Bethany Pentecostal Church in Plymouth nourished it.

"He called me long before I heard
Before my sinful heart was stirred,

But when I took Him at His word
Forgiven, He lifted me!" [11]

Divine Providence had set the steps in motion, and provided the enabling circumstances, organisations, and people to seal His calling on my life.

CHAPTER FIVE

The Big Six

In September 1968, I, along with a group of five other students entered the Sixth Form (Humanities/Arts group) at the Montserrat Secondary School to begin two years of study leading to the University of Cambridge Advanced Level certificate in English Literature and History. (There was another group of students pursuing science subjects). I was not registered for the English Literature examination but shared in the often intense classroom discussions about the literary works which the other five were studying. I developed such an interest in the discipline that I subsequently ended up taking the subject at university and doing well in it. We were all also preparing to sit the General Paper which was a compulsory essay examination designed to cultivate critical thinking on contemporary global issues.

We called ourselves the "Big Six," and we acted as if we were. This group of four boys (Leroy 'Rocky' Martin, Josephus 'Junior' Lewis, David Edgecombe, and Oral Howes), along with two girls (Jacinta 'Jo' Thomas and me) was to form a deep and lasting bond which has spanned more than half a century. We all graduated together in 1970, and despite going our different ways, separated by vast oceans, we all reconnected through social media somewhere around 2010. To this day, we remain in regular online communication on at least a weekly basis. Once a month, we have a virtual evening gathering via an online meeting platform, and these gatherings often last well into the night. There is always stimulating conversation about current events, reminiscences about teenage escapades, and supportive dialogue about our individual journeys in between. We all learn from these meetings and leave motivated to become better versions of ourselves in some way.

Several factors contributed to the exceptional and uncommon bond which we developed. One of these was an idea (I don't remember whose it was) for us to put on a play during our Sixth Form journey. Classroom space was scarce at the Montserrat Secondary School of the 1960s, and so we were allocated space in the school library. There, we were surrounded by books of all genres. We sought to find a play with no more than six main characters, preferably four males and two females. We scanned the bookshelves and dug into numerous boxes of books which were stored in the library. We had some free periods each day – sessions when we had no timetabled formal classes, but were expected to engage in private, or group, study. We used some of those free periods to read the plays which we found, mostly authored by British playwrights which were the ones available to us at the time.

When we came across *The Dover Road* by A. A. Milne, we knew we had found our play. It had the right mix of characters for our small cast, and it was a brilliant comedy which captured our imaginations. David had a passion for theatre, and under his direction, we pursued the staging of this play. His skill, enthusiasm, and attention to the fine technical and aesthetic details of theatre energised all of us, and kept us working despite the pressure of preparing for the Advanced level examinations at school. We were all in. The high degree of mutual respect which flowed between us, and the genuine friendship we had developed as a cohort produced positive energy. Motivated by a common passion and purpose for this undertaking, the Big Six successfully staged "The Dover Road" in our school's auditorium in 1969.

We did other things that were unheard of for teenagers at school at that time in Montserrat. Some of the teachers raised their eyebrows, but they need not have. Respectful of our parents, and of our elders (including the teachers), we did not get up to any major mischief. Sure, we celebrated our friendship by sneaking out to get professional photographs taken together. These photos are now an iconic record of the uniforms and style of the 1960s at the Montserrat Secondary School.

There was one incident which cemented in my heart and mind the bond of support and loyalty which came to define the Big Six. One afternoon, on my walk home from school, I stopped at a small shop that sold groceries in one section, and liquor in another. I do not recall what errand took me there, but it was not unusual for me to pick up the odd tinned item or other necessities such as sugar, flour, or salt. I was inside the shop waiting to be served, when I heard some loud talking outside, and in walked a well-known local man who hailed from the north of the island, and went by the nickname "Muggy".

Muggy walked into the shop, clearly in an agitated state, and without any warning, took the two or three steps to reach where I was standing at the counter. He threw a huge backhand across my face. The force of the blow split my lips and knocked me down. My lips quickly became swollen. The other persons in the shop, startled by this unprovoked occurrence, rushed to my aid, and helped me back to my feet. Someone drove me the short distance to my home. The police were informed, and they advised that I was the third person who had been assaulted by this man during the same day. All the usual police formalities were done with the guidance and support of my mother, as I was barely seventeen years old.

A few days later, I was summoned to court to attend the hearing in the criminal case of the assaults against me and others. Nervous and anxious, I arrived at court in my school uniform, as it was a school day. As I was seated to await the hearing, I turned around, and to my amazement, there were some of my Big Six school mates sitting in the courtroom, dressed, like me, in school uniform. They had come to give moral support, and it was so deeply appreciated. A feeling of warmth still courses through my chest even now in recalling the incident. For someone who struggled with feelings of alienation and inferiority, this display of loyalty and friendship was huge.

My classmates and I had fun together outside of school. I remember one beach picnic when I brought a whole chicken that my mother had roasted, and we devoured it. But we were also serious students who held study sessions together, often in a room at Oral's home. We laughed a lot, to the consternation of his parents and older siblings. His mother was unconvinced by our explanation that we were laughing at history jokes. But we were. Truly.

For example, our Tudor British history course included the impacts of King Henry VIII's quest to have his first marriage annulled to expedite his marriage to the young, beautiful Anne Boleyn. Thomas Wolsey, the English cleric who became Henry VIII's chief adviser, was tasked with obtaining the annulment from the Pope. However, despite his favour with the Pope, who appointed him a cardinal, Wolsey was unable to procure the annulment which the King so desperately wanted and expected Wolsey to deliver. Falling into disfavour with Henry VIII as a result, Wolsey was charged with treason, and sentenced to death by beheading.

Studying this episode in British history, we recounted a satirical comment which suggested that by the time the distinctive cardinal's red hat arrived for Wolsey, he might no longer have a head to wear it on. We mulled over the hand of fate which resulted in Wolsey dying of natural causes before he could be executed. The discussion grew more animated, and the sarcastic twists of the commentary we were reading drew loud laughter. Of course, this was soon followed by firm knocking on the door to find out what kind of studying could possibly be generating so much mirth.

After high school graduation, we followed our individual career paths, which took most of us away from Montserrat. All of us went off to university, and some of us migrated to the United States, Canada, or other Caribbean countries at various times. The Big Six group lost touch, but there were always some of us, David for example, who made every effort to keep tabs on his classmates.

David pursued theatre arts and management and became the successful Artistic Director of the world-famous Reichhold Center for the Arts in the US Virgin Islands, drawing stellar acts from as near as the US and Jamaica, and as far away as South Africa, and Russia. When an international choir had to cancel its appearance as feature act of the month at the Reichhold Center in September 1994, David invited my choral group *Voices*, a performance choir from Montserrat, to fill the slot. He had attended one of our concerts the year before and had privately shared with me his delight at the talent of the group, and the quality of our programme and performance. However, it must have taken some persuasion on David's part to get *Voices*, a virtually unknown choir, onto the Reichhold stage in substitution for a previously advertised, and internationally renowned choir. His faith in the group was not misplaced, and I can still remember how he beamed with pride at the overwhelming response of the audience during and after the performance.

David also roped in some of his Big Six former classmates to participate in several of his theatrical productions. One of these, entitled "Strong Currents," was entered into the second World Black and African Festival of Arts and Culture in Nigeria in 1977. Of course, as we recall, David the theatre director was not David the Big Sixer. Rehearsal was serious business, and he was a demanding director.

Jo moved back to her native St. Vincent and subsequently attended university in Canada. She had a successful career in both airline management and insurance in St Vincent and has also been actively involved in Toastmasters International.

Rocky pursued a career in law, and practices in the United States. He is also a superb, expressive singer who has returned to Montserrat from time to time, and entertained audiences as a soloist.

Junior developed a passion for the culinary arts as a child and pursued a career in hospitality management both in the Caribbean and in Canada.

Oral studied business management and went on to head a significant revenue-generating agency in Montserrat, before relocating with his family to the US, where he entered the business sector. A brilliant gospel singer-songwriter and pianist, he has served in the music ministry of his local church and produced stellar concerts for the benefit of the community.

I have been a teacher for most of my adult life, and, apart from an eleven-year stint of work and study in England, I am the only 'Big-Sixer' still residing in Montserrat.

David's sudden passing in late 2021 broke a unique circle that had remained tight knit, loving, and affirming for over fifty years. Who could have foreseen that a disparate group of teenagers thrown together at the Montserrat Secondary School would have developed an enviable friendship which has not disintegrated or become stale over time, but which, in our later years, continues to support, inspire, and bless us all. We have shared personal triumphs and tragedies, successes and setbacks, and have benefitted from each other's counsel, encouragement, well wishes and prayers.

Through God's enabling grace, our Big Six group has created a non-judgemental space where we can share personal challenges with each other, receive a wealth of sound advice, and discuss perspectives from biblical and experiential standpoints. Our meetings are cathartic, and in a blame-cultured world where so many persons fear to expose their vulnerabilities, this is such an incredible blessing. As one 'Big-Sixer' put it after a recent gathering, "God is good to us, making us a blessing to each other." Another expressed the same sentiment, "I can't believe how kind fate is, to bring us back together in our senior years to support each other."

That I, who struggled with feelings of inadequacy and yearning to belong in my youth, found myself unexpectedly interconnected with Jo, Junior, Rocky, David, and Oral, has been life-changing. My self-worth was solidly reinforced through this exceptionally cohesive group of classmates. This was no coincidence. Once again, God, in His omniscience, orchestrated the right people, under the right circumstances, at the right time, and now, with the right technology, to provide a virtual oasis of support for each of us. The shared warmth, love and support have made a significant impact on my mental, moral and emotional well-being. I am consistently held accountable for prioritising important relationships and investing in them, even sacrificially, if necessary.

These former classmates and enduring friends continue to inspire me. During the summer of 2023, we held our very first Big Six reunion. It was the first time some of us were seeing each other, face to face, in more than fifty years. It was a heart-warming time of reflection, reminiscing and thankfulness as we celebrated our friendship. Until the end of time, we will always be the Big Six.

CHAPTER SIX

I Didn't Choose Education

As a child, I wanted to become a nurse when I grew up. I had lived around medical facilities of some kind all my life. Grandad, with whom I lived until he passed away, was a surgeon. Mummy was a nurse, and so was her only sister, my Auntie Gwen. Each of Mummy's three brothers had married a nurse. During our trips to spend school vacations in Montserrat with Mummy, Beverley and I lived at the Matron's house at the edge of the Glendon Hospital compound in Plymouth. Most of the small Glendon Hospital staff in the early 1960s would have experienced Matron Dewar's little daughters dressed up in white caps and aprons, pretending to be nurses and hanging around the children's ward.

While my own career dreams became somewhat scattered in the clouds after I entered secondary school, Beverley's ambition seemed carved in stone. After she left school in 1970, she attended the Tercentenary School of Nursing in Barbados, qualified as a Registered Nurse, and returned to work in Montserrat. Shortly afterwards, she proceeded to the United Kingdom where she underwent training to become a State Registered Midwife, followed by certification in Neo-Natal Intensive Care. Her career was a remarkable one, and I deeply admired her practical approach to nursing, along with her strong professionalism, empathy and care.

I cannot recall any single instance or situation that drew me away from nursing as a career goal. But I did drift along without any decipherable pull towards a future career for several years. Then, in my Fifth Form year (Year Eleven), I developed a strong interest in social work. One of my dear friends, Lazelle Howes, was a student at Oral Roberts University (ORU) in Oklahoma, USA. The reports from Lazelle were riveting. They were not only about the campus, the studies and the programmes. They were also about the environment of worship and fellowship, and the spiritual growth she was experiencing. I knew by then that I wanted to gain a qualification to prepare me for social work, and I knew that I wanted to attend ORU. As I neared the end of my secondary schooling, I sent off for the application pack and contemplated my future.

Eventually, the application pack arrived, and I carefully scrutinised it. I realised, with a sinking heart, that the costs were far beyond the reach of Mummy's financial capacity. According to the information received, it did not appear that I would qualify immediately for a scholarship. Perhaps if I had discussed the matter with someone much more knowledgeable, there might have been a way. But a huge cloud of disappointment descended on me, and I decided to keep it to myself. I had Advanced level exams to prepare for at school and could not handle such a huge distraction at that time.

My dream of social work now crushed, I found myself approaching the end of my secondary schooling without any career direction. I decided that while I contemplated my future, I would seek clerical or secretarial employment with the government or a non-governmental agency, whichever one offered a position first.

In early July 1970, just a few days before I graduated from secondary school, my exams were over, and I attended school as usual. For some reason that evades me now, I went across to the auditorium, and en route, I happened to see that a notice had been placed on the students' notice board right outside the auditorium. Curious, I stopped to read it. It was an invitation from the Education Officer in the Ministry of Education to school leavers who were interested in becoming teachers at the primary school level. I had never really given teaching any serious thought – actually, no thought at all. Sure, like most of my friends, I had 'played school' with my sister as children often do. But becoming a teacher was not on my radar – until I read that notice. I read it again, and proceeded on my way, but the thought kept nagging me.

The next day, I re-read the notice which invited eligible school leavers to contact the Ministry of Education to indicate interest. I could not shake the thought, "What do you have to lose? Who knows, you might just like teaching." After telling Mummy about it, I contacted the Ministry and indicated my interest. Soon afterwards, I was invited in for an interview to discuss my eligibility and qualifications. I was selected for a few weeks of orientation training the following month, and then offered a probationary position as an uncertificated teacher at the Maple Leaf School in Plymouth. I was eighteen years old.

I have often reflected on this unexpected encounter at school, where I was led to enter a career path which I had not contemplated. God had plans for my future and cleared all other career ideas out of my way, to lead me into the one for which I was predestined.

God's plans were better. I can honestly say that I was created to be a teacher. At the Maple Leaf School, I had superb mentors who believed in me and painstakingly guided me. Reuel Francis, a qualified and experienced educator, stands out as the most helpful, and as we taught year groups which were close in age and ability, I learned so much about the practical aspects of teaching. He was great at Mathematics, while I was quite good at English Language. Occasionally, he taught Mathematics to my class, while I taught English Language to his. It was a win-win partnership. I also benefitted from other teaching legends such as Miss Florence Malone, and the larger-than-life 'Teacher Hess' Meade. We taught under the headship of Headmaster Alfred Lee, a strict disciplinarian with a strong, but approachable, personality.

This year of internship opened my eyes and my mind to consider teaching as a career, at least in the short term. At the end of my first year, I was offered a scholarship to Erdiston Teachers' Training College in Barbados, to qualify as a trained teacher, with certification from the University of the West Indies. And so it was that, in September 1971, I travelled to Barbados and enrolled at the prestigious Erdiston College.

The two years spent at Erdiston were extremely impactful in several ways beyond teaching. The back gate of the College opened onto a street just yards from The People's Cathedral, a large Pentecostal church. I had some acquaintance with the church already, as I had met several young people from this congregation who visited Montserrat on an evangelistic mission, and I had stayed connected with some of them. So, I sought fellowship at the church and was accepted. I joined the choir and participated in the open-air evangelism programme and the Sunday School. I was "adopted" by the Holford family, a wonderful Barbadian household full of camaraderie, spirituality, and love, and I spent almost every weekend with them. As a choir member and soloist, I had many opportunities to develop my musical expression and abilities. I also travelled to other Caribbean islands as a soloist with evangelistic ministry teams from the church.

At Erdiston College, I boarded with the most marvellous roommates and experienced a rich and rewarding campus life. I thoroughly enjoyed the study programme, and did well, particularly in the practical teaching aspects of the course, where we interned at various schools for several weeks at a time. I gained much confidence in the practical methodologies for creating enabling environments in which students at all ability levels could be motivated to learn. However, although I had begun my career in education at the primary school level, I realised, especially from my internships, that I really enjoyed teaching at the high school level. As a result, I included courses aimed at teaching the post-primary age groups. In 1973, I graduated from Erdiston College with distinctions in the Practice of Teaching, Education and History.

On returning to Montserrat, I was re-assigned to the Maple Leaf School. I knew that I had found my calling to be an educator and wished to concentrate on teaching at the secondary level. For this, I needed to specialise and earn at least a bachelor's degree. I was hungry to pursue further education and applied for a scholarship to read for an undergraduate degree at the University of the West Indies. English and History were my subjects of choice, as I was most comfortable in the Humanities. I had passed Biology at ordinary level certification, but had not pursued qualifications in any other science subject.

I must say a word about my connection with Biology as a school subject. I had been exposed to the subject only briefly during my first three years of high school in Antigua, and I enjoyed it. But when I transferred to school in Montserrat, Biology was not offered for most of the years I was a student at the Montserrat Secondary School. However, when I entered the Sixth Form, two teachers from Barbados joined the faculty. Mr and Mrs Ferguson were science teachers, and Mrs Ferguson taught Biology. Her personality was endearing and infectious, and both she and her husband clearly enjoyed teaching and mentoring students. As I had no other science subjects in my 'O' Level qualification portfolio, I decided to take Biology, and subsequently earned a certificate in that subject.

When I visited the Ministry of Education to make my formal pitch for a scholarship to university and was asked what my areas of study would be, I stated English and History. The Chief Education Officer was a career educator. She was responsible for ensuring that the schools employed teaching professionals who could expertly deliver the subject modules required to cover the curriculum at all levels of the school system. It was clear to her that I wished to transition from generalist teaching at the primary level to specialist teaching at the secondary level. But now she was looking at me with a shocked expression.

"English and History?" she queried, as though she thought she had not heard me correctly. "English and History?" she repeated, in a tone of clear disappointment. "You don't want to study anything else?" she challenged me. It was clear that there was no pressing need for teachers of English or History.

I knew instantly that English and History were not going to win me a scholarship. My survival instincts swiftly kicked into gear.

"Biology," I said. It was blurted out, with no meticulous thought behind the words. It was the only other subject that entered my mind in that critical moment. Never mind that it was not a subject I had considered pursuing at any higher level. I had already said it - the horse had already bolted from the proverbial stable.

The Chief Education Officer drew a breath and seized the offering. "Yes," she said, in a tone of relief. "Biology is needed."

After a further brief discussion, I was told that I would be contacted if my application was forwarded by the Ministry to be considered for a scholarship. Several weeks later, I was advised that I was among the successful candidates for a scholarship to the University of the West Indies to pursue a bachelor's degree, with a significant component in Biology. I was granted study leave to pursue undergraduate studies.

I entered the University of the West Indies at Cave Hill, Barbados in September 1974, on a full scholarship. It was a Canadian government-sponsored scholarship, with one of the best-funded grants available to Montserratian students. Having satisfied matriculation requirements for the Faculty of Arts and General Studies (now re-named the Faculty of Humanities and Education), my major would be English Literature, but a significant component for each year of my studies would comprise of a full module of Biology. I was allowed to make up course credits with a few elective courses in History. I also decided to attend some classes in Chemistry, to ensure that I had the background needed to manage the biochemical aspects of the Biology modules.

Since the Biology course was non-negotiable, the only drawback was that I had to wait until the timetables were finalised for the Faculty of Arts and General Studies (from which I would choose the desired courses in English Literature and History), and the Faculty of Natural Sciences (for the Biology components) to ensure there were no timetable clashes. I carefully chose the English Literature and History courses and waited with bated breath for the timetable release at the beginning of each of the three academic years. Through God's grace, I had no clashes at all until my final year, when there was a tutorial clash which was swiftly and providentially sorted out.

In 1977, I graduated with a bachelor's degree with the required components in Biology, and my desired components in English and History. In the process, I had also accumulated an adequate knowledge of Chemistry and Mathematics to manage the biochemical and computational aspects of the Biology course. There is no question that Divine Providence was aligning the various elements to fulfil the masterplan for my life.

Returning to Montserrat in the summer of 1977, I was appointed to teach Biology in the upper forms at the Montserrat Secondary School, and I introduced Biology at the Advanced level for the two-year Sixth Form programme. In subsequent years, I also taught Creative Writing in the lower school, and English Literature at Advanced level to the Sixth Form. I taught for three happy years, enjoying the nature of the job, as well as interactions with my students and faculty colleagues. I was, indeed, in a career which brought out the best in me, and provided so many opportunities to motivate, encourage, nurture, and mentor young people with diverse backgrounds, interests, and abilities.

Each day brought new challenges, and new hope. I was fortunate to have the oversight of a particular group of students in the Fourth Form who were adventurous and enthusiastic about having a well-rounded experience at school. These students formed a teen club, and over a weekend, I took them camping. We had planned a range of activities geared towards the interests of these adolescents, including talks on aspects of emotional and physical health, spiritual discussions, and several leisure activities. The highlight of the camp was a free concert, of a very high quality, which the students put on for persons living in the community where the camp was held. Over forty years later, these students still speak, with some pride, of this concert and other activities of the teen club. It was all their initiative, and I was blessed to be a part of it.

While I greatly enjoyed my work as a teacher, I had a desire to pursue postgraduate studies in education. However, this was a pipe dream. How would I fund it? What course(s) would best assist my development as an educator? I started looking at courses run by the Open University in the UK and decided to explore this option. I soon found out that the Open University courses I desired were not available to persons living outside of the United Kingdom or Europe. To pursue the course, I would need to travel to the UK or Europe. Another disappointment in my career dreams. I let the dream die.

However, another situation was brewing on the personal front, which threatened to shake my emotional peace. I had yet to learn how to appropriately handle disappointments in relationships, and the degree of concern which this situation generated was most unwelcome. Professionally, I was a successful teacher and cultural practitioner, but my personal life felt disorganised.

All this was happening at a time when there were other challenges to grapple with. My mother had been diagnosed with cancer and had developed a serious condition associated with the form of the disease which assailed her. As debilitating as this was for her, she remained stoic, but the reality of her condition was most distressing. She desperately needed further medical attention which was not available in Montserrat. However, this was financially out of our reach. Beverley and I had both recently returned to Montserrat from studying abroad and had not amassed the required level of savings. Mummy herself did not have enough savings to cover the huge medical costs overseas. None of us had any form of health insurance at that time. It was a dilemma.

But once again, God had a plan. A relative visited us in Montserrat. He had recently sold some family land and had arrived to present us with a cheque to cover our portion of the land. The hope, the relief we felt was enormous. God not only knew of our need. He had already prepared the way before the need became apparent. Furthermore, it was recommended by the doctors that my mother seek medical attention at the University Hospital of the West Indies in Jamaica. This was a perfect arrangement, since Daddy's family lived there, and my Aunt Ruby lived within walking distance of the hospital. Mummy was able to travel to Jamaica, where she was admitted to the University Hospital for treatment and was graciously attended to by loving and most generous in-laws. Beverley and I travelled to Jamaica on two occasions to visit Mummy in the hospital, and we were so warmly embraced by the extended family there.

The prognosis on Mummy's condition was not good, however. She was admitted to hospital in Jamaica in January 1980, and she succumbed to cancer six months later. Beverley and I were numbed by her passing. It was as if we had been sucked up in a huge vacuum. It was an extremely difficult place to be in.

One Sunday soon after Mummy's funeral, I simply felt overwhelmed, trying to cope with the loss of my mother, as well as with the emotional rollercoaster in my personal life. And I made an ill-thought-out decision. I would leave Montserrat to get away from it all, and I would go to England. But even in that situation, God went ahead of me, and my sojourn in England for eleven years proved to be another experience of Divine Providence in operation in my life. I relate those events and circumstances in a later chapter.

For now, I will only say that God, in His grace, allowed me to find long-term employment in England, in a position that would redound to my benefit in remarkable ways. It also provided me with training in many of the components of social work, which had been my dream career until teaching came along. Additionally, several opportunities were placed in my way to work with people of all ages, from vulnerable children to the elderly, persons with physical and mental challenges, and adolescents coping with single parenthood. My teaching qualifications and experience assisted me in obtaining these and other part-time evening and weekend placements, so that I was able to fund postgraduate degree studies.

When I was ready to return to Montserrat in August 1991, I found that my old job as Biology teacher at the Montserrat Secondary School had just become vacant, and the Education authorities were seeking for a suitably qualified teacher to fill the position. What perfect timing! My post had been quickly filled when I left for England by someone who was coming to Montserrat from abroad. And now, that person was leaving Montserrat to pursue studies abroad, just as I was deciding to return to the island. So, on returning to Montserrat, I stepped back into my old job.

Everything was different, however – different Principal, faculty, administrative staff, and of course, different students. Most of all, the examining institutions for the school certificate examinations had changed – from the Universities of Cambridge and London to the Caribbean Examinations Council. This meant new examination syllabi, new coursework components, new examination structures.

My new Principal, Mrs Camilla Watts, was already known to me, a woman I greatly admired and respected. As expected, I found her to be most helpful and inspiring, with deep spiritual values and strong interpersonal skills. A mission-driven individual whose slight frame belied a profound strength, she was nevertheless the epitome of empathy, undergirded with deep commitment to the well-being of both her students and her staff.

In addition to my duties as Biology teacher for the upper forms (Forms Four to Six) at the Montserrat Secondary School, I was given the responsibility of teaching Biology to students in the Third Form at the Junior Secondary schools. This meant that I had to travel, especially to the Salem campus which was a few miles from the main campus where I was based. The assignment was not at all tedious, however, as I enjoyed teaching the subject so much. Besides, at the end of their third form year, students selected the subjects which they would pursue to certificate level. It was a thrill to introduce them to the study of Biology, and to see them immerse themselves in the discipline and then select it for further study. I therefore resumed a most meaningful journey in education.

A few years later, however, I discovered that there were people within the wider public service who felt that I could make a useful contribution to the service beyond education. It was a great surprise when, in 1996, I was invited to attend an interview with the Public Service Commission. As part of a succession planning strategy, the Commission had been tasked with interviewing individuals within the public service who might, with appropriate training and mentoring, be eventually able to succeed in more senior administrative positions. I, along with several other public service employees, was being considered for this training.

I had no desire to end my teaching career, but one does not simply turn down an invitation to interview when one has no idea where the future will lead. So, I attended the interview. Some of the questions were in unfamiliar territory, given my limited experience of public service employment besides teaching. I had a lot to learn about mainstream public service operations and procedures, but I was interested, and determined to embrace this new challenge. I considered myself trainable.

Several months after this, I learned that I was to be transferred from the Montserrat Secondary School to the Department of Administration (the 'Human Resources' division of the public service) to undergo orientation and training. With just weeks to go before the ending of the academic year, and in order not to inconvenience the operations of the school during that period, it was determined that I would attend the Department of Administration for training two days each week until the end of June 1996. Thereafter, I would be transferred to my new posting, and the school would need to find a new Biology teacher.

Divine Providence was again at work. Nearly one year before this, in July 1995, the Soufriere Hills volcano in the southern part of Montserrat had begun erupting. Life was becoming chaotic, with residents of the areas closest to the volcano being required to relocate from time to time. Montserratians had started to leave the island, and the trickle became a steady stream when, in 1996, the eruptive phase accelerated, causing the evacuation of the eastern and southern villages of the island. Many people without access to alternative accommodation were forced to shelter in schools and churches in the northern 'safe' zone, and the British government aided those who wished to relocate to the UK or to other Caribbean territories. As schools in the north of the island were turned into shelters, and those in the other areas forced to either close or to relocate to other temporary accommodation, many parents took or sent their children overseas for schooling.

In September 1996, several teachers who had spent the summer holidays abroad, returned to Montserrat to resume employment for the new school year. However, due to volcanic activity, the closure of schools in evacuated areas, and the relocation of children overseas, several teaching posts were no longer required. Some teachers were reassigned to other functions within the public service. Others relocated overseas. And so it was that Divine Providence had already prepared an alternative career path for me even when I did not realise it would be necessary.

I remained in employment within the mainstream public service until April 7, 2007, when I celebrated my 55th birthday and attained the official age of retirement. In the meantime, I had served as Chief Training Officer for a brief period, and then in two Permanent Secretary postings, all of which I thoroughly enjoyed. I worked with some outstanding public officers, both senior and junior, and each of them contributed to my learning and my job satisfaction.

By Divine Providence, I had the privilege of sitting at the feet of outstanding mentors such as Mrs Claudia Roach, Miss Alfreda Meade, Mr C.T. John, Mrs Elaine White-Samuels, and Miss Clemence Fergus. And there were so many others – I quickly learned that every worker had valuable lessons to impart if one was willing to learn. Some of the most important procedures were, in fact, taught to me by an outstanding office attendant. I will forever be grateful to these people who were willing and ready to assist in my training and development.

I was not ready to completely abandon teaching, however, and neither was teaching prepared to abandon me. Secondary school students and their parents still reached out to me long after I had left the education system. So, I continued to assist students who were preparing to write the Caribbean Examinations Council certificate examinations in Biology. I had never liked giving individual instruction in these situations. I found that students sitting these examinations profited more from group tutoring, and so I suggested that if the students brought along other classmates who were seriously interested in getting extra help, I would be happy to provide a class one afternoon each week. We all benefitted – the students got extra help and passed their exams, and I remained current in my knowledge of the Biology course content and methodology.

As retirement approached, I was often asked what I was going to do after I left the public service. The answer was always the same – return to teaching. One person to whom I gave this response stifled a laugh and remarked that I needed to have my head examined. Others frowned and asked if I was serious. The level of salary paid to teachers made the profession less than appealing. There were many persons who could not understand why I would wish to return to a profession which was, in their opinion, undervalued, especially considering the disciplinary issues and increasing complexity of the job. But I had developed a love affair with education, and I was determined to seek avenues to return to the profession.

So it was with great joy that I accepted appointment as School Development Adviser at the St Augustine Catholic Primary School, less than three months after my retirement from the Montserrat Public Service. Just two years later, the position of principal at the school became vacant, and my application for that post was approved. This was one of the most fulfilling occupations I had ever had up to that time. The opportunity to work with a superb team of teachers and administrators to build on previous gains and successes was enormous. The work of the school received accolades, and the academic and athletic performance of students were highly commended year after year. With great support from parents, teachers, benefactors and the wider community, I was able to develop a number of initiatives at the school. These innovations included the establishment of an annual science fair. This kindled an excitement around science projects and discovery by students as well as their parents, who were drawn in by their children's enthusiasm. Funding for the establishment of a computer laboratory, and landscaping of the school grounds to provide a safer recreation space for the pupils, enhanced the facilities. The annual multimedia presentation exercises and the creation of a school song enriched the school experience.

A few years later, I felt it was time for me to retire from full-time employment. In September 2013, after handing over to a new school principal, I settled down to begin enjoying my freedom from employment. But once again, teaching was not done with me. One month later, I was asked whether I would consider teaching the Caribbean Advanced Proficiency Examination (CAPE) course in Caribbean Studies at the Montserrat Community College. Already one month into the new school year, the college was still without a substantive teacher for this mandatory course.

As I perused the Caribbean Examinations Council's (CXC) syllabus and course requirements for the Caribbean Studies modules, I saw that this multi-disciplinary course covered the history, culture, geography, and development issues of the Caribbean. These were all content areas with which I was familiar, and my public service placements had provided me with a good grounding of the main development issues facing the Caribbean. I said yes, and at 61 years old, began an exhilarating part-time teaching journey into the deep and fascinating area of Caribbean Studies. I enjoyed a great deal of success in this endeavour, and despite a further "retirement" after eight years in this position, I have continued to assist in preparing students for their examinations by occasional guest-lecturing and supervision of coursework projects. In addition, I have continued to tutor groups of high school students preparing for their certificate examinations in Biology.

Teaching has, therefore, defined most of my adult life, even though I was called away from the education sector into the wider public service for a few of those years. In hindsight, I perceive that I was being providentially prepared for a life in education after retirement. The experience gained within the wider public service provided a comprehensive knowledge and understanding of how Government and the Montserrat Public Service operated. I was also blessed with opportunities for overseas training to lead and manage public service delivery and human resource development. These courses allowed me to develop awareness of the skills involved in international training facilitation, since I observed the methods and training resources of the facilitators as much as I learned the course content.

Together with my school teaching and public service experience, I was able to build on the methodologies, content and resources learned to develop training interventions for both public and private sector organisations in a range of topics. These include customer service, time management, work ethics, primary school science teaching methods, team building, public service registry procedures, codes of conduct for the public service, and professionalism at work. Out of this has grown a part-time freelance training design and facilitation service, which provides excellent opportunities to assist the development of persons of varying ages, stages, and sectors in the Montserrat community. This has marvellously enhanced my life after retirement.

Teaching is, understandably, not everyone's idea of an ideal career. It was certainly not mine until opportunity beckoned. And, like many educators, I found that most times, rewards do not come pouring in quickly. Satisfaction is often delayed. But the rewards, when they do eventually come, are heart-warming.

I received a letter from a student whom I had met in the Third Form of secondary school and who I believed was inappropriately placed in the B (middle ability) stream. This young lady, of Montserratian parentage, had come to live in Montserrat with her grandmother. She had been placed in this stream according to her assessed ability, but she was producing essays and classwork at a level which suggested higher ability. Based on her performance, I felt that she would be more appropriately situated in the top stream. I had brought my observations to the authorities but did not find much support. I suggested to the student's guardian that she also make a request for her ward's placement to be reviewed.

Thankfully, at the start of the next academic year, the student was re-situated in the A stream, and she went on to write the Caribbean Secondary Education Certificate examinations. She returned overseas before the examination results were received, and I had the absolute joy of locating her and telling her, by phone, that her results were among the best on the island in that year. Her letter to me, several years later, said:

> *I just wanted to drop you a very long overdue note of thanks and appreciation for absolutely everything you were as my teacher, all those years ago! It takes great skill to empower a child to genuinely be interested in a subject in which hitherto there was nil interest! Thanks for being a great support – you may not have realised how much it meant... I felt you genuinely cared and wanted me to do well, and sometimes that was the only thing that kept me focused and going!*

Subsequently, she wrote again to let me know that she had completed graduate studies, qualified as a solicitor and was practicing law in her country of residence.

There have been several other stories, but just two examples will suffice. About thirty years ago in the US, I happened to meet one of my former Biology students, who was now a fully qualified physician. During our brief conversation, she said to me, "Miss Dewar, I am a doctor today because of you." More recently, another former student who had attended one of my weekly after-school tutoring groups remarked to me that I was the first teacher who helped her to really grasp the subject of Biology, and thus, to decide on a career in medicine. That former student is now a senior health official in her home country.

Throughout my career as an educator, my students have been the centre of my world. From the hugs of the kindergartners at the St. Augustine Primary School, to the texts of appreciation from the graduating high school Biology students and the Caribbean Studies students at the College, my heart has been filled to overflowing with joy. Students have challenged me with their insatiable quest for understanding of their world, environment, and the issues of life. This has invariably led me to further research and reflection, which in turn have increased my understanding and thirst for knowledge, and application of that knowledge to life situations.

One of my college students decided to undertake research on attitudes to the native language of Montserrat. As I supervised her research project, I became deeply interested in the topic. As I checked her sources and evaluated the strengths of her arguments and evidence, I started conducting research of my own. A year or so later, after this student had graduated, I continued to research the topic, and in March 2016, I was invited to present my research at the annual St Patricks Day Lecture organised by the University of the West Indies Open Campus in Montserrat. In presenting the lecture on *The Importance of the Montserratian Creole Language in Forging a National Identity*, I gratefully acknowledged my student who had inspired me. A condensed version of that lecture formed the introduction to my first published book, a collection of poetry in the Montserratian language, entitled *Wha Marmie Say.*

Teaching opened revolving doors of opportunity, satisfaction, and reward, enabling me to cultivate and hone several skills, as well as to build and maintain lasting relationships. These have enriched my life beyond measure. This was my true calling, discovery of which was surely the work of Divine Providence. Without a doubt, the chief sources of inspiration in my journey as an educator have been my students, and I can only hope that I have inspired them as much as they inspired me.

CHAPTER SEVEN

A London Sojourn

In July 1980, my life was at a crossroads. As I related earlier, my mother had passed away after a battle with cancer, and I was numb from the experience of losing her. I was also in an untenable relationship, but with the loss of my mother, I did not have the strength or will to deal with relationship issues. I was just drifting along. One Sunday afternoon, mulling over my situation, I had what I thought was a brilliant idea – a solution to the problem. I wanted to pursue a master's degree in Education. Why don't I go to England for a year, I thought. Get away from it all, get my masters' degree, and then return home with a fresh take on life.

I confess that I did not think it through. The idea flashed into my head, and that was it. The next day, I went to see the Chief Education Officer to tell her that I was resigning my teaching post and going away to study. She looked at me and flatly informed me that I was required to give three months' notice. However, in discussion, I found that I could apply for a year's study leave instead of resigning, since I wished to pursue a one-year masters' degree course. Another amazing thing happened - over the ensuing weeks, a qualified Biology teacher moved to Montserrat to join her husband and was available to take up the teaching post I was going to vacate. My application for study leave was approved. I contacted a friend in London who arranged temporary accommodation for me until I got settled.

And so it was that on September 21, 1980, I left Montserrat to travel to England. Arriving in London the following day, I listed the three most urgent things I needed to do:

1. Apply for admission to the masters' degree programme at the Open University.
2. Find a job.
3. Find a church.

To my dismay, I found that I could not access a relevant course at the Open University at that time. This was a huge blow. It was the reason I had applied for study leave. I had not obtained sufficient information before I travelled to London, and classes had already started. This was before the availability of Internet and electronic mail, so everything had to be done via the postal service. I was advised that there were options available to commence the course at the next intake. That, at least, was hopeful, but left me with an unplanned amount of free time on my hands.

When I realised that I would have to defer my masters' degree studies, I also knew I needed to quickly find employment. My host felt that I should sign on for welfare benefits at the local Department of Health and Social Services to have some income while I sought employment. However, a mysterious set of events occurred.

About three weeks after I arrived in London, I had a strange sensation in my limbs, and some numbness in my lower legs. My host hurriedly took me to her doctor, who ordered some tests at the Whittington Hospital, which was very close to where I was staying in North London. On my arrival at the hospital I was again examined, and admitted as a patient. The medical staff there conducted even more tests to try to make a diagnosis. I grew more concerned as each day passed, and the symptoms grew worse. I could feel a touch to the upper parts of my legs, but in my lower legs there was no sensation whatsoever. My education in Biology led me to believe that there was some neurological explanation for my strange condition, but the doctors could not arrive at a diagnosis.

After a day or two of inconclusive tests, a lumbar puncture was scheduled for the third day of my hospitalisation. I had read a story several years before of someone undergoing a lumbar puncture. I seemed to remember that there was excruciating pain involved, which the patient described as a horrifying experience.

I tossed and turned and cried all night at the thought of the procedure which awaited me the next morning. The nurses were concerned, and asked why I was so distressed. I told them what I had heard about lumbar punctures, and they did their best to reassure me that it would not be painful, and that these diagnostic procedures had been tremendously improved and modernised. I was unconvinced, and spent a sleepless night, terrified beyond description, and feeling a profound sense of despair. Even prayer did not relieve my distress at that time.

The next morning, filled with deep trepidation, I steeled myself for the ordeal that was to come. The nurses were right. The procedure was very skilfully done, not at all painful or uncomfortable, and was quickly completed, to my great relief.

Divine Providence was at work once again, orchestrating events and situations for my good. During my hospitalisation, a young woman was admitted to the ward and placed in the bed next to mine. She introduced herself, and we started talking. When I mentioned that I would be seeking employment after my release from hospital, she told me about an employment agency in central London which she highly recommended. She encouraged me to apply for an agency job, at least until I found more permanent employment.

I was discharged from hospital a few days later, on a Wednesday, with my condition still undiagnosed, but with reduced symptoms. I thought I needed at least a week's rest to see if my symptoms would completely clear up. However, I did not know how long it would take to get an appointment with the agency, or a job placement. So, I called the agency the very next day, Thursday. To my surprise (and some dismay), the agent who took my call asked me to come into the office for an interview the very next morning, Friday. I attended the interview, taking my qualification certificates. It turned out that there was an opening for a temporary full-time administrative clerk at a large architectural firm in Central London. I was offered the job on the spot, but they needed me to start immediately.

On the following Monday morning, I started work at the architectural firm. There I was introduced to a team of incredibly supportive co-workers who quickly showed me the ropes. The firm was re-organising its filing system for architectural documents and required an assistant for this task. It was quite methodical work, not difficult but requiring diligence. As it turned out, given the expertise and helpfulness of my colleagues whom I could consult as needed, it was quite relaxing, and allowed me to earn, even while continuing to recuperate from my recent illness.

About two weeks after starting work with this firm, a friend of my host visited the house where I was staying and brought with him a copy of a popular weekly London newspaper. As the newspaper lay on the dining table, I had a look at it. On the back pages, an advertisement jumped out at me. The Greater London Citizens Advice Bureaux Service needed an Advice Worker. I had never heard of such an occupation, nor of the organisation. But the job seemed very interesting. Full training was offered, and the salary was attractive. Best of all, the office was located within the borough of Islington where I was currently living. While I did not yet have the local knowledge of Islington, I felt that I more than met the other basic requirements, and I considered myself a quick and willing learner.

I rang the advertised number, requested the application pack, carefully completed the documents, and submitted them to the address supplied. Very soon after, I received a letter inviting me to attend an interview at a central London location. I checked out the address to ensure that I could find it easily on the appointed day, and I turned up for the interview. Less than twenty-four hours later, I received a telephone call from the lead interviewer, and was offered the job. An offer letter arrived in the post within a couple of days, to which I immediately responded with a formal acceptance.

I later found out that there were two hundred and forty applicants for the position. I had recently arrived in London and must have been much less knowledgeable than most, if not all, of the other applicants about the organisation, or about life and customs in London. Realising that this might be the case, I did not hide the fact during the interview, but highlighted my education and work experience. I underscored my willingness to contribute to teamwork, and my ability and intention to learn and to seek advice where I was uncertain. This was an entry level position in Advice Work, and I was teachable. I thanked the architectural firm and the employment agency for the enjoyable job they had provided and gave the required one week's notice.

I went to work at the Highbury Corner Citizens Advice Bureau (CAB) on December 8, 1980, and embarked on a nearly eleven-year journey that led me to become an experienced lay advocate in the County Court. Some of my clients were facing legal action for debts owed to housing authorities, utility boards and credit card companies. My work also included representing clients in their appeals against refusal of Social Security welfare benefits. In addition, diverse matters such as no-contest divorces, citizenship applications and appeals, change of name instruments, and so much more, were part of my portfolio. The bureau had an elaborate information system which we kept updated on a regular basis. In addition, there was an exceptional cadre of experienced legal practitioners and other experts at the end of a telephone whom we could call upon to assist the clients who came in.

The work was tremendously fulfilling and enjoyable. We made a significant difference in our community by providing information and advocacy to persons from all walks of life, ages, social statuses, belief systems, lifestyles and nationalities. Looking back, I marvel at the sequence of events which led me to finding a job via an unexpected encounter with another patient in hospital, and then to fulfilling my teenage dream of doing social work via a newspaper which was providentially placed within my view. I also learned that the organisation offered a retirement pension plan, which I had the option of joining. While retirement seemed a long time in the future, I decided to join, and became a contributor right from the start of my employment.

The training courses offered by the CAB service were second to none and provided numerous opportunities to travel all over the UK. Also exciting were the opportunities to work in a variety of bureaux in London, to provide cover for staff absences. I established strong working relationships among my colleagues within the Islington bureaux and received favourable reviews.

When the manager of one of the Islington bureaux went on sabbatical leave for several months, I was tapped to act as manager of that bureau. None of the workers at that bureau were Black. I already had a great relationship with the staff, but I was not sure how the clientele would react to a Black manager. There were, indeed, a few eyebrows raised, but the stint proved most enjoyable, and gave me the experience of managing a bureau. I was encouraged to apply for a permanent managerial position in the future. When my manager at Highbury Corner retired a few years later, I did apply for the vacant position. My application was successful, and I began a new appointment as Manager of the Highbury Corner Citizens Advice Bureau.

I had not given up on my goal of earning a master's degree in education which had been deferred. However, after I obtained the Advice Worker position at the CAB, I decided to pursue the training which the organisation provided, and to extend my stay in the UK. After discussing the matter with the Chief Education Officer in Montserrat, I resigned from my teaching position. I never wavered in my desire to return to reside in Montserrat, but I also could not take for granted the opportunities provided in London at that time, which I saw as being of potential benefit when I returned to the country I called home.

My bureau undertook an outreach project with some schools in the borough of Islington, and as I had both the appropriate teacher training, and the interest, I was delegated to go to the school to lead a class of students in Citizens Rights Education. As I carried out this duty from time to time, I saw how important such exposure was to young people, and could be for young people in other countries too, including Montserrat!

Several ideas came together at that time. I had been exploring the taught masters' degree programmes offered by the University of London's Institute of Education. The University was within easy travel distance from my office, and the classes were held in the evenings. There was an extensive library which was open on Saturdays to facilitate students in full-time employment.

One course caught my attention. It was titled *Rights in Education.* According to the brochure, it was a multi-disciplinary programme that explored the law, philosophy, psychology, history, and politics of education, and the ways in which concepts of human rights, equality and justice impact educational policy. I was intrigued and read everything I could about the course. The more I read, the more attractive it seemed to be. And the more I saw how this programme would provide me with a well-rounded approach to delivering education, whether in the UK or in Montserrat. It was a much more suitable course than the one I had originally contemplated pursuing when I arrived in the UK.

There were only two hurdles that I could see. One was that I did not have a degree in either the social sciences or education, which was a pre-requisite for the *Rights in Education* course. The second was that I did not have the money to pay for the course under the terms specified by the university.

But God had a plan. My application to the university was not rejected. The Admissions Office responded to my application by advising that I needed to undergo a qualification assessment. This assessment was through an essay of a set number of words, which was to be submitted with full referencing within a specified time. The essay topic was entirely new to me – it dealt with law as an instrument of reform or repression. I spent as much time as I could in researching and forming evidence-based arguments on the topic. After writing and re-writing, I finally had a draft which I felt addressed the topic. I submitted my essay, and a few weeks later, received an unconditional offer of a place on the two-year Master of Arts course in Rights in Education, to start in September 1988.

There were still a few months to go before the date of registration, when the course fees needed to be paid. And here, too, Divine Providence stepped in. A lady, whom I met in

London, happened to mention the name of a social care agency that placed persons with suitable experience as temporary part time support staff in care institutions. These care institutions included residential care homes for vulnerable children, homes for the elderly, homes for at-risk mothers and babies, and homes for persons with physical challenges. Most of these placements were part-time staff cover during the daytime and on weekends, while others required sleep-in overnight duties.

I applied to the agency, passed the vetting procedures, and was soon placed for evening and weekend cover at a home for at-risk mothers and babies. Then I was placed at a children's home. Over the first two months or so, I provided relief cover for several residential care homes, and after this, some of these homes called me directly and added me to their regular night and weekend staff rotations.

I still got calls from the agency, so I learned to juggle emergency placements with my regular cover shifts and my full-time job at the CAB. I often had to carry an overnight bag to work as I was frequently called out for an emergency sleep-over and had to head straight for a residential care home immediately upon leaving work. Many weekends were spent at work. I both learned and earned during these placements, and when the time came for me to register for the two-year master's degree course, I had saved enough money to fully fund my studies. Once again, God's timing and plans for me had proven to be much better than my own.

At the same time as God's plans for my employment and education were taking shape, I was also seeking a home church where I could worship, and a congregation with whom I could fellowship, and serve as the Lord led.

The family I stayed with had some relatives who were Christian believers, and we quickly became friends. By the second week of my stay in London, they had decided to assist me in finding a place of worship and took me to two churches. The second one was the Sandringham Road Evangelical Reformed church where the pastor and his wife were Montserratians. The leading elder in the church was the eldest brother of my Howes family schoolmates, and the eldest son of my pastor in Montserrat. Several of the church members were Montserratians. I immediately felt at home there.

The services were quite different from those at the church I attended in Montserrat. They were more formal, strictly elder-led services. Only time-honoured hymns of the faith were sung, with organ accompaniment instead of multiple musical/percussion instruments. The Tuesday evening Bible studies and Thursday night prayer meetings were attended by most of the members and given similar importance to the Sunday morning and evening worship services. I benefitted from the solid expository preaching of the Word, which had centrality in the Sunday services, as well as the robust and joyful singing of the lyrically rich hymns. The methodical Bible studies that explored theology and doctrine helped me learn to rightly divide the Word of Truth (2 Timothy 2:15, NKJV).

The church was filled with young people, many of whom I quickly befriended, and the church members were gracious and welcoming. I had several invitations to various homes for Sunday lunch, where I got to know many of the church families quite well. In fact, after I had found a job, one family invited me to come to their home after work on Tuesdays and Thursdays for a meal, and from there, it was a short walk to the church for Bible study or prayer meetings. I knew I had indeed found a church home in London, and a family of believers. It was clear to me that all of this was providentially arranged.

Each service and each interaction with the elders and members of the church only served to strengthen my conviction that I was in the right place for that time in my life. They understood only too well some of the pitfalls of the newly arrived in London, especially ones like me without family members close by to assist in making decisions.

The pastor, Reverend Thomas B. Tuitt, had initially gone to the UK to attend a conference in the mid-1950s. He was well known and respected as a Christian believer in Montserrat, active in the Pentecostal church. In London, he was beseeched by Montserratian migrants to become their pastor, as so many of them did not find immediate acceptance among London congregations. Sensing that this was God's will, Pastor Tuitt became the leader of a small gathering of mainly Montserratian Christians in North London. Soon, the numbers multiplied and outgrew the modest hall where they were meeting, causing them to move to larger premises in Hackney, East London.

In the UK, Pastor Tuitt encountered vigorous expository preaching from a wide range of preachers, as well as books by renowned Puritan expositors and historical research documents on the early church fathers. He was an avid reader and collector of books on Christian theology, and as he studied and learned, he taught his congregation. Through years of solid Bible study, the congregation embraced the biblical foundation of the doctrines of grace, and with uncompromising, vibrant Bible-centred preaching, the church became thoroughly evangelical and reformed.

The congregation of the re-named "Evangelical Reformed Church" continued to expand and outgrow building after building. I attended as many services and meetings as I could, as the Word-centred ministry met the hunger within me to learn more of God, His plan of salvation, the teachings of Scripture, and how to live daily as a Christian in practical terms. My heart was stirred by the words and beautiful music of the old hymns of the faith and the faithful preaching of the Word. Like the Bereans, we were encouraged to search the Bible for ourselves to see if the teaching we were receiving accorded with Scripture. We were taught to examine all Scripture in context, and to allow Scripture to interpret Scripture. The Tuesday night studies took us into systematic theology and thorough research on the nature of God and other major themes of the Bible.

I also discovered the benefit of reading to my own spiritual growth. Pastor Tuitt introduced me to books such as *The Sovereignty of God* by A.W. Pink and works by theologians such as Charles Haddon Spurgeon and Dr Martyn Lloyd-Jones. These authors, as well as some prominent Puritan writers, were of immense benefit to my spiritual growth and understanding. Psalm 25:5 was coming true in my life – "*Lead me in your truth and teach me, for you are the God of my salvation; for you I wait all the day long*" (ESV).

It was, however, a steep learning curve, and I had much to learn. Several of the beliefs which I had simply accepted before were now being confronted by the Word of God. I struggled with this and had many questions. But week after week, I grew in my understanding of the doctrines of Scripture, and the importance of applying them to daily life, even those which were culturally inconvenient to the present time. I had to deal firmly with my own pride, as I learned to submit modern ideas and culture to the authority of the Bible, rather than the other way around. I got involved in the music ministry of the church, and thoroughly enjoyed playing the lovely pipe organ for Sunday services and directing a small but eager youth choir.

During this time, I was also in search of long-term housing, as the accommodation I had moved into on my arrival in London was temporary short-stay housing. When I found my church family, I also found that Divine Providence had already catered for my accommodation needs. I was offered rental accommodation in an apartment within the home of an elderly couple who were members of my new church family. This was a particularly good arrangement, as it was well located, and allowed me to continue to learn about life in London while not being completely on my own. My landlord and landlady treated me as their own daughter, and I learned much from them.

Eventually, I was offered the opportunity to purchase the leasehold on an apartment within a most desirable neighbourhood, close to buses, overland trains, and the London underground. The bus route took me directly to my office. The apartment had just become vacant, and the owner was also a member of my church family. Although I had only been in the UK for a short time and had no assets, my employment with the Citizens Advice Bureaux Service, a national organisation, enabled me to secure a mortgage from one of the largest building societies in the country. This was a huge blessing. I had great accommodation not only for myself, but I was able, over the remainder of my time in London, to provide accommodation for several relatives who visited, as well as for others who migrated to London and needed a place to stay for the short term.

Some of the enduring memories I have of the encyclopaedias which Mummy had purchased for Beverley and me as children, and which I read over and over like story books, were the beautiful pictures and descriptions of the countries of the world, their cities, people, culture, and unique features. How I dreamed of travelling abroad, to these faraway countries and cities which seemed magical, enchanting, and... so out of reach. But here I was now, living in London, with its expansive transport system and proximity to Europe, which provided many opportunities to travel.

The internal information bulletins which came to my office at the Citizens' Advice Bureau, regularly announced group tours arranged by one of our colleagues in the organisation, which meant that I did not have to travel alone. My church also planned occasional bank holiday outings within mainland UK. And as I became more familiar with the British transportation system, I explored further.

I went on day trips within the UK: to Brighton and Southampton in the south, Weston-Super-Mare and Bristol in the west, Coventry, Birmingham, and Leicester in central England, Liverpool and Blackpool on the north-western coast, and Great Yarmouth, Ipswich, and Margate on the eastern coast. There were also mini vacations to Llandudno in Wales, Lucerne in Switzerland, Rouen in France, and Amsterdam in Holland. These travel opportunities, a childhood dream come true, added so much diversity and cultural significance to my lived experiences.

On the weekend trip to Amsterdam, while strolling with a friend on a path overlooking the canals, we discovered from our guide map that we were only two blocks away from the home of the late Anne Frank. She was a young Jewish girl whose diary documented her family's life between 1942 and 1944 as they hid from Nazi persecutors in an attic in Amsterdam. She was caught and transported to a Nazi concentration camp where she perished in 1945, just a few months before her fifteenth birthday. *The Diary of A Young Girl* by Anne Frank was published posthumously and is one of the world's best-known books of that genre. I had been enthralled in reading the book and had also recently seen a film based on the life of this brave young girl. I was ecstatic to have the opportunity to visit the house and the attic where Anne Frank and her family had hidden. We arrived at the venue just as a tour was about to start. It still is one of the highlights of my travel experiences.

During my eleven-year residence in the UK, I returned to Montserrat for short holidays on three occasions, and each time, I realised how much I missed my island home. When I returned for the third time, in December 1989, the island was in recovery after being devastated by Hurricane Hugo three months before. Electricity was being restored village by village, and, in fact, was restored in the area where I was staying with my sister just as we sat down to dinner on the evening of my arrival.

Although the hurricane had caused serious disruption to the schools, when I contacted the Principal of the Montserrat Secondary School to see if I would be able to conduct research surveys for my master's degree dissertation, my request was met with utmost positivity and grace. I was so awed by the resilience of the residents. Despite the destruction all around, the school officials and teachers generously accommodated my research during my short vacation on the island. I was due to complete the master's degree course the following year, in mid-1990, and I determined that, God willing, I would return to Montserrat in the summer of 1991.

The next two years were full of both providential blessings and nail-biting decision-making, some of which I deal with in other chapters. I passed the dissertation and examinations and was awarded the degree of Master of Arts in Rights in Education from the Institute of Education of the University of London. It was around the same time as I was promoted to the position of Manager of the CAB in which I worked, upon retirement of the previous Manager.

Despite these successes, however, I still felt certain that I should return to Montserrat, and therefore, I began the preparations to do so. I decided to apply for a year's sabbatical leave, so that I would not be burning my bridges in London until I was sure that I had made the right decision to return to Montserrat. I applied for a teaching position at the Montserrat Secondary School, preferably to teach Biology in the Upper school. I also contacted a real estate company and put my apartment up for sale.

There was a nerve-wracking lull after my apartment was put up for sale, when there seemed to be no movement whatsoever. I had a few months to go before my departure from the UK, but my apartment had been newly renovated, with a lovely bathroom, modern well-equipped kitchen with new cabinets and ample storage, and central heating throughout, and it had been expected to sell quickly. Every day when I left home to go to work, I ensured that the whole place was spic-and-span with nothing out of place. There were some viewings, but no offers.

As the days passed, my anxiety grew, and some nights were almost sleepless. What if my apartment did not sell? What if the agent was not expending effort on my sale? What if the seller's market was drying up? And on and on and on.

One night, it all came to a head. There were about two months left before my departure to Montserrat. I went to bed with great trepidation. I tossed and turned for hours, feeling almost suffocated by fear and anxiety. If it was God's will for me to return to Montserrat, as I felt it was, why was this last critical hurdle so challenging? The weight of despair was crushing. I climbed out of bed and dropped to my knees in tearful supplication. I cried out to God, poured out all my anxiety and distress, and laid my fear and my questioning at His feet. I placed my situation in His hands. A peace like I had never experienced before descended over me. I arose from my knees, with faith, hope, and that enveloping peace, and I slept. In those wee hours of the morning, I again learned the power of prayer.

This experience was to bolster me on so many occasions in the future when I was faced with decisions or difficult situations. I knew, beyond any doubt, that God answers prayer according to His will and purpose. Just a few days later, I received a reasonable offer for my apartment, which I accepted.

The buyer wanted a short closing period, so with a few weeks left before I was due to travel, I had to feverishly pack up, clear the apartment, and find alternate lodging. Again, God had already provided for this eventuality. During my master's degree course, I had met a Jamaican woman who, I discovered, lived diagonally across the street from me – no more than twenty paces in distance! She agreed to let me stay at her home for the short period before I travelled. I had already arranged to ship some of my household belongings, and so I did not have far to move the few remaining personal items that I planned to take with me to Montserrat.

On August 20, 1991, as I boarded the flight from London taking me back to Montserrat, my home, I left behind the life I had enjoyed in London. Eleven years' worth of education, study, work, and Christian discipleship traversed the Atlantic Ocean with me. My master's degree certificate, together with a letter confirming a one-year leave of absence from my job were carefully packed in my hand luggage, along with a small notebook containing the addresses of most of the members of the Evangelical Reformed Church of Lauriston Road, Hackney.

My church family meant the world to me. Together, we had gone through years of soul-searching reflection as we sought to make our calling and election sure, as 2 Peter 1:10 exhorts believers to do. Just a few months before, we had mourned the loss of our beloved Pastor Tuitt, who, on April 18, 1991, had attended the weekly prayer meeting as usual, and then, after he returned home from church, had passed on to Glory during the night. Immediately prior to his passing, he had been preaching a series of sermons on Ezekiel 36:26 & 27:

> *I will give you a new heart and put a new spirit within you; I will take the heart of stone out of your flesh and give you a heart of flesh. I will put My Spirit within you and cause you to walk in My*

> *statutes, and you will keep My judgments and do them (NKJV).*

This encouraging and timely admonition which our pastor had so carefully expounded to us, was one which I needed to have solidly embossed in my mind and on my heart as I left behind a spiritual community which had fed and nurtured me during my sojourn in London.

When I had first arrived in London, I heard a song which echoed the dismal coldness, and potential loneliness which some folk said would await me in this city I now found myself in. Certainly, the opening events of my sojourn in London were not encouraging. *The Streets of London*[12] with its haunting melody, spoke to the inward fear of being all alone, and the feeling of emptiness and alienation in unfamiliar and expansive territory. But the song also invites us to look outward, and to realise how much we have to be thankful for. The song still speaks to me, clearly and strongly, of how much my life was grounded and guided by Divine Providence while living and working in London.

CHAPTER EIGHT

Who Buys Montserrat, Buys Me!

Montserrat is a small British Overseas Territory in the Caribbean, and despite residing in four other countries for extended periods between childhood and adulthood, this is the only country I have ever called home. I was enchanted by the history and pageantry of England, as a child. Then, on a visit to the US when I was twelve years old, I found the glitz and glamour of New York City - the wide avenues, huge stores, and spectacular entertainment - thrilling. During my secondary school years, several of my school friends had left to join parents and other family members in the big cities of the US and the UK. The trek had continued into my adulthood. And while I had opportunities to visit many big and exciting countries, I was glad to return home to Montserrat.

This island provided an idyllic environment for growing up. In 1959, Mummy moved back to Montserrat where she had grown up, and the only country she called home (although she was born in St. Kitts). Beverley and I looked forward to spending every single school vacation with her. There was just something special about Montserrat. Maybe we had a bit more freedom on this little island to spend days at our friends' homes or they with us. Mummy had colleagues and friends with children our age, who embraced us fully.

Those were the days when the village helped to raise the child. We were as careful to mind our manners and to be on our best behaviour when outside our home as we were inside our home. Better not let your parents hear that you had misbehaved. If you were lucky, you got a good telling off and a severe grounding. But you never knew if a slipper or wooden spoon was close at hand. Sometimes a strong bare hand did the job equally well. Beverley and I were very fortunate that Mummy did not believe in spanking therapy. We did have a few close calls, though, but one look, one softly spoken admonition (more often than not it was just your name spoken in that soft tone together with raised eyebrows), and that was always enough. Those were the days!

Montserrat was the country that I associated with the happiest times of my life. It was the setting for so many opportunities, and I love this land. My mother used to say, "Whoever buys Montserrat, buys me." I grew to understand why, and to feel the same way. The secondary education system provided me with a sound foundation on which to build a fruitful and entirely satisfying career. And even though the island's geographical location and geological features made it susceptible to natural disasters, living in Montserrat was, in my view, living in paradise. That was, and still is a blessing. I will always be grateful that God, in His sovereign will, carved out a place for me in Montserrat. Looking back, I can trace His hand in the many opportunities granted, challenges faced, and lessons learned from life on this island.

During my eleven-year residence in England, I looked forward to returning home periodically for vacations, and each time I did, I just knew deep in my spirit that Montserrat was where I wanted to be. So it was with eager anticipation that I set about my studies and prepared myself for my eventual return, if that was God's will. What I hoped would be my last return for vacation was approaching when Hurricane Hugo struck the island with ferocity on September 17, 1989. I was due to travel to Montserrat just three months later. The BBC news bulletins were full of headlines about this tiny British colony which had been severely devastated. Most communications were down, and this was before widespread internet services. Everything was by post or telephone.

I tried contacting my sister in Montserrat to see how she had fared but could not reach her at all. I was in a near panic after several days with no contact. Eventually, my cousins in Antigua took a boat to Montserrat to try to find her. They reported back the next day that she was well, but like everyone else, had suffered major damage to her accommodation and possessions. Over the next two weeks I was able to restore contact with Beverley, and continued my plans to travel to Montserrat.

When I arrived in Montserrat in December 1989, I was shocked by the ruins I saw throughout the island. But I also saw the strength and resolve of the people of my island, who were rebuilding brick by brick, shingle by shingle. The traditional practice of marooning was strong. This was a custom where people in the community helped each other to build or repair houses, reap crops, or do any other task where many hands made light work. As the local saying went, "Today for you, tomorrow for me." A clear recognition that we were all in this together.

The devastation of the hurricane could not mar the inner beauty and toughness of the Montserratian spirit or the friendliness and helpfulness of the people. It cemented my desire to return and contribute to rebuilding. After my too-short vacation, I returned to my life and job in London and set in motion the plans for what I prayed would be a permanent return to Montserrat. To test the waters, I had obtained one year's leave from my job in London. And so, I journeyed back to Montserrat, just in time for the start of the new academic year at the Montserrat Secondary School, where I resumed my career as a Biology teacher.

Despite its small size and population, there are many opportunities to serve the community in Montserrat. There was quite a variety of organisations – local, regional, and international in scope, and wide in range and reach - so I could choose the ones in which I could participate fully, and soon I had a busy schedule. Most of all, I enjoyed my job as a teacher. Divine Providence had led me to this career and had brought me back to it.

I need not have had any concerns about being able to settle back into life in Montserrat. Shortly before my sabbatical leave was up, I wrote a letter to the CAB Service, which had provided such stimulating employment during my stint in London, and I resigned. It seemed clear to me that I belonged in Montserrat.

That belief was shaken to the core three years later, when seismic signals showed that the Soufriere Hills volcano, in the southern mountain range of the island, was becoming active. I was not in Montserrat on July 18, 1995 when the volcano began erupting. I had travelled to Trinidad to participate in a Caribbean Examinations Council marking exercise for the examinations in Biology. When I got back to the hotel from the marking centre that evening, I was met by colleague markers from other islands, who had arrived back at the hotel before I did and had heard the news on the Trinidadian radio and television stations. I was stunned, and rang my sister, who confirmed the news. Over the next few days, I could think of little else but tried to apply myself rigorously to the work I had gone to Trinidad to do.

Speaking with my sister frequently, I learned that residents were leaving Montserrat and seeking shelter in Antigua and other islands, out of fear of the eruptive activity. She was also going to travel to Antigua with her son and wait to see what would unfold. I decided that I would join them in Antigua when the marking exercise in Trinidad was completed. And so I did. We monitored the situation several times daily from the radio reports. The villages located near the volcano had been evacuated, and school and church buildings on the northern side of the island were turned into shelters to accommodate the displaced villagers.

After several days in Antigua, both Beverley and I were anxious to return to Montserrat. Despite the chaotic housing situation, given the danger from eruptions, we needed to secure important documents and make informed decisions about work (Beverley was the local office manager for an international NGO). A friend of ours had offered us temporary accommodation in a rented apartment in the north of the island, and so we returned to Montserrat.

At the airport in Antigua, there were just a few of us boarding the Leeward Islands Air Transport (LIAT) flight for Montserrat. When our flight was called, it was clear that some people were unimpressed by our travel plans. As we walked toward the gate to show our boarding passes, there was an unveiled comment from a man seated in the departure lounge to his travel companion.

"Look at them," he said, with an accent and in a vernacular rooted in the Caribbean. "Volcano eruptin' down in Montserrat, and they goin' to Montserrat."

The next year was spent in a state of uncertainty and increased alertness, all related to the volcano. Every day, we ensured that we had the required evacuation bag packed with important documents, medication, clothing, and other essentials in case we had to move swiftly away from volcanic hazards. We listened to the volcanologists and other officials via radio and watched the "mountain" from a distance. We rapidly gained an education in basic geology, volcanology, and associated vocabulary. Our lives revolved around the volcano. During periods of heightened activity, we sometimes had to move away from our home. But for most of the time, we were able to remain at home in Dagenham, on the outskirts of the capital, Plymouth.

One evening, while we were at home, we heard the volcano rumbling. There had been some ashfall as well in the area where were lived. While the radio had not carried any imminent evacuation orders, Beverley and I were concerned at the heightened level of activity. But, apart from the crowded shelters, we had nowhere to go. Then the telephone rang at about 9 p.m. We recognised the voice on the other end of the phone. It was a dear friend, Gloria. She lived in the northern "safe" zone, and had already taken several people to shelter in her small home together with her family.

"The volcano is acting up," she said. "It is not safe for you to be there. Come." Gloria's voice was firm. Her words were not a suggestion. They were a command!

Beverley and I quickly retrieved our packed evacuation bags, dragged two small mattresses, some bed linen, and Beverley's young son, and dashed out to our motor vehicles. We headed to the north, to Gloria's house, joining a steady stream of vehicles also heading to safety in the north of the island. When we got to Gloria's house, we found that she had piled her living room furniture in a corner of the room. This created enough space for us to set our mattresses on the floor so we could get as comfortable a night's rest as was possible. In the morning, with the light of day, we thanked Gloria and returned home.

Over the next several months, volcanic activity was again in high gear. Beverley and I temporarily evacuated our rented accommodation in Plymouth several times. We spread mattresses on the floors of friends' homes and offices, only to return home at daybreak to shower, dress for work, and attend to the myriad chores of each day. And then to get back to friends' floors at sunset.

Admittedly, there were times when the constant back and forth became wearying, and we stayed put at home, risking it all just for some semblance of stability. But stable it was not, as we discovered on more than one occasion. There was a week when at regular intervals, the volcano would send pumice stones and debris of rockfalls explosively into the air, and the force was sufficient for them to reach even the border areas of the northern safe zone. We swiftly learned to time these events, and to hasten well into the safe zone, just beyond the reach of the hazard. We waited there on the roadside in our vehicles, until the raining volcanic missiles had stopped falling and it was safe to return home.

One evening, weary of the constant scampering, we dragged our feet. The volcanic episode started, and we heard a few light "pings" on the shingle roof. But then it grew in intensity and volume, and we realised that we needed to get our motor vehicles away from the area, otherwise the windshields could be cracked by the force of the projectiles. We made a mad scramble for our vehicles and drove as fast as we could to a safer place. Returning home, when the episode was over, Beverley and I looked at each other and sighed over the chaos our lives had become. We were thankful that despite the falling stones, we had not suffered any damage. That cyclical episode ceased as suddenly as it had started.

Many people who lived in the areas deemed potentially hazardous, were opting to join a British government-assisted relocation scheme and move off the island, mostly to the United Kingdom. But many others opted to stay in Montserrat for the time being and rented property in the northern safe zone of the island. The north was not as highly developed as the areas under threat in the east or the urban centre, so available housing was limited. Beverley and I were uneasy about remaining so close to Plymouth, with the hazards and imminent evacuation orders. We knew we needed to decide swiftly. Our search for alternative accommodation did not turn up many possibilities. Someone, it seemed, always got there before we did.

At the end of November 1995, Beverley got a telephone call from our friend, Gloria. She had heard of a house that was being renovated, and she thought that it would be very suitable for us. But, she cautioned, we had to act swiftly. Beverley called and was able to reach the owner who set up an appointment for us to view the house the next day at 10 a.m. We thought we would have a look at the house to determine whether it was suitable for us. However, early the next morning, Friday December 1, 1995, a mandatory evacuation order was announced. All residents of Plymouth and surrounding areas (including Dagenham where we lived) had to leave within forty-eight hours. Realising the gravity of the situation, I quickly re-prioritised our budget and withdrew what I hoped would be sufficient money to make an acceptable rental deposit on the house we were due to see at 10 a.m.

When we got to the house, located in the northern safe area of Olveston, we learned that other people had been there before us and had offered rental deposits in the hope of securing the house. The owner was a man of principle, and, mindful of our appointment, would not rent to anyone until Beverley and I had viewed the house. Divine Providence had been at work. We offered a deposit there and then, rented the house, and drove back to Plymouth to begin packing our essential belongings. We moved into the Olveston house with only a few minutes to spare before the evacuation deadline.

We spent Christmas 1995 in evacuation in Olveston. By New Year's Day, volcanic activity had subsided sufficiently to allow us to reoccupy the Dagenham property in Plymouth. This had been our third substantial evacuation, and Beverley and I were weary of the process of what was, literally, moving house. We mulled over the situation, and the days stretched into weeks. We were still paying rent for the house in Dagenham, as well as for the one we had moved to in Olveston. Our salaries could not continue paying for two homes. Which one was it to be? We discussed the situation at length, as we both worked in Plymouth, within walking distance of the Dagenham house. However, after a lot of deliberation, we decided that it was too risky to give up the Olveston property, as the volcano was still very active. By now, the month of February 1996 was ending, and rents for both houses were due in advance on the first day of each month. We decided to give up the house in Dagenham and informed the landlady.

As it turned out, we were Divinely led. Just four weeks after we gave up the Dagenham house, volcanic activity heightened again, producing potentially deadly pyroclastic flows which travelled swiftly down the flanks of the volcano. Another mandatory evacuation order was made for Plymouth and its environs. Had we returned to Plymouth, it seems almost certain we would have had nowhere to go. No one was permitted to live in Plymouth after that day, and eventually, massive pyroclastic flows obliterated the capital city and the areas surrounding it. Photographs of the location of the house where we had lived in Dagenham revealed that nothing was left standing.

Looking back, as we did many times since then, both Beverley and I were enveloped in awe as we realised that even amid the scramble for rental properties in the safe zone, God, in His omniscience, had prepared a house in Olveston for us, revealing it to us at the exact moment we needed it. A year later, Beverley and her son relocated overseas due to her urgent medical needs, but I continued to live in the rented house in Olveston for another five years.

During that time, volcanic activity continued. There were nail-biting moments when thick ashfall blotted out the sun. Thick mud of heavy ash combined with rainwater covered house roofs, yards, and roads. Cleaning up after ashfalls was a tedious, backbreaking job, but every single time, God sent help in amazing and often unexpected ways.

I received calls from friends and relatives overseas, urging me to leave Montserrat. But I was one of the fortunate ones. I had accommodation in the northern safe zone, and I had a job that I loved, teaching Biology to students writing the Caribbean Examination Council's certificate examinations.

As the school building was in the evacuated area, classes for the Fifth Form were held in the unfinished basement of a house still under construction in the safe Olveston area. There were no windows installed, and the floor consisted of sheets of plywood placed over the hard ground. My Biology class was too large for the small rooms, so I stood in a doorway between two rooms and taught my class which was divided between the rooms. The students in one room could not see those in the other room, but they could all see me.

There was no laboratory to conduct any Biology experiments, so I selected the most essential ones, and the students came in smaller groups to my home to conduct these practical exercises. Due to the unavailability of equipment and limited resources, the experiments had to be improvised and modified. The students, thankfully, were as committed as I was, and they did well in their exams. I believed then that there was work for me to do in Montserrat. My resolve was unshakeable.

Beverley and I had always dreamed of owning our own home. Our parents had not been homeowners. But we wanted to put down roots in Montserrat and secure housing for our retirement years. Shortly before her death, many years before the volcanic crisis, Mummy had bought some land at Foxes Bay, which Beverley and I inherited. We had an architect draw up house plans according to the existing covenants for the area. A few years after I returned to Montserrat to reside, we made an appointment to see the manager of one of the leading mortgage lending institutions, as we wished to start building.

We met a stumbling block as soon as the interview began. Although Beverley and I were in good jobs (she as the local manager of an international non-governmental agency, and I as a well-qualified graduate teacher) neither Beverley nor I were earning enough money, we were told, to build a house with three bedrooms. This we considered to be our minimum need as Beverley had a ten-year-old son to be accommodated as well.

There was one glimmer of hope presented to us, however. If we started the building process using our small savings, and got the foundation built, we could then re-apply for a mortgage to finish the house. Beverley and I left the mortgage interview despondent, as we were both less than comfortable using our limited funds to start building, with no firm agreement to assist us in finishing what we were told to start. We discussed the possibilities but decided to wait until we could secure a mortgage. Friends recommended another mortgage scheme, run by a government-owned agency, but we found no comfort in that alternative plan either.

After the volcanic eruptive activity began, the areas in the East, South, and the capital of Plymouth and surrounding areas all became part of the Exclusion Zone, and no one was permitted to live in those areas. Foxes Bay, where our land was situated, was part of the Exclusion Zone. That area became uninhabitable due to the threat of volcanic activity. Located in an evacuated area, the buildings, roads, and other infrastructure have fallen into disrepair and neither electricity nor running water has been restored.

What would have happened to our investment had Beverley and I decided to start building in Foxes Bay, and then taken on a mortgage to complete the building? We would have had to leave our newly built home to the elements, and, as happened to others whose insured homes were in the Exclusion Zone, the insurance company would have paid out only a fraction of the assessed value of our home. Divine Providence had intervened in the form of a most unwelcome denial of a mortgage, and the unfavourable alternative, to which we were reluctant to commit. God had guided us in this situation. How apt is the statement of Proverbs 16:9, which reminds us that "*The heart of man plans his way, but the LORD establishes his steps*" (ESV).

Indeed, I was soon to discover that God had other plans. The extended period of volcanic activity and resulting evacuations of the capital Plymouth and many villages, created a critical demand for housing. Those persons who lived in the evacuated areas and who wished to remain in Montserrat were either squeezed into private housing with relatives and friends, or had rented the limited housing available in the north of the island, or were living in temporary shelters in churches and schools.

Among several solutions provided by the government, with aid from international donor agencies, was a "soft" mortgage scheme. It was available, under specified terms and conditions, for relocated persons on a limited income to purchase land and build a house of not more than 1,200 square feet. Beverley had, by this time, relocated with her son to England, but wanted to return to Montserrat as soon as she was able to, housing, schooling, and health permitting. I needed a three-bedroom house to accommodate us. But I did not even have land in the northern safe zone.

Early one morning, in February 2001, there was a knock on the front door. It was not yet 7 a.m. Wondering who could be coming to visit at that early hour, I opened the door to find a gentleman with whom I was acquainted, on the doorstep, with a golden smile. My greeting matched his smile. He was going to work but had stopped by to speak with me. He got straight to the point.

"I hear you are looking for land," he said.

"Wow," I said, not expecting this line of conversation. "Yes, I am."

I had asked a few people if they knew of any land for sale in the north of the island, but up to now, I had only had one lead, and that land was out of my price range. Land had become a scarce commodity, and the price had escalated.

"Well," he said, "I just heard about some land for sale, so I came to tell you about it." He gave me the contact details, and I thanked him, as he headed back to his vehicle.

I wasted no time contacting the person whose name I had been given and made an appointment to see the land. It was quite close to where I was living at the time, in the same area of Olveston, and with a more affordable price tag. I felt as if God had led me to this land. The seller and her agent were highly professional and made the process swift and smooth. I obtained a loan to purchase the land. With the title deed in my hand, an architect friend designed a home within the specifications of the soft mortgage scheme, and I was approved for a mortgage. I hired a building contractor, and another friend of mine, who had overseen several building projects of his own, offered to supervise my building construction. All of this happened by April 2001. On December 31, 2001, I moved into my newly built home in Olveston. God had truly given me the desire of my heart. Divine Providence had moved obstacles out of the way and replaced them with opportunities. God's plans were better.

Montserrat is a culturally rich community. There are vibrant masquerade and creative dancers and folk choirs. The spectacular costume parades at the annual Christmas festival give way to heritage displays and intellectual conversations during the St Patricks Festival in March. Local drama, storytelling, literary festivals, culinary and artistic exhibitions, and concerts of all descriptions are also part of the cultural product of the island. There is a wealth of opportunity to explore one's own creativity in this setting.

There is also that most expressive medium of communication – the Montserratian native language. Based on the English code, it has its own grammatical structure, peculiar vocabulary, and turn of phrase. Replete with local proverbs, innuendos and figures of speech, the Montserratian language is truly a potent vehicle for communicating the Montserratian experience.

As a teenager, I loved hearing and speaking Montserratian. I keenly read and appreciated the work of other Caribbean writers, such as Jamaican Louise Bennett and Trinidadian Samuel Selvon, who had both overcome initial literary prejudice, and were now successful authors using Caribbean languages. With their example, I was emboldened to start expressing my own poetic thoughts in the Montserratian language.

Much encouragement came from my mother, who was never too tired to listen to my poems, and from Sir Howard Fergus, himself a literary giant. (Sir Howard, my former Latin and History teacher, who also encouraged me in my spiritual journey, had, in 2001, been conferred with a knighthood by Her Majesty Queen Elizabeth II for his outstanding service to Montserrat.)

I received many invitations to present my poetry at both official local and regional occasions, as well as at more informal local events. Several persons asked permission to perform my poetry at Montserratian heritage events or other cultural celebrations in the US, UK, and the wider Caribbean. Eager for the Montserratian language to receive due recognition, I was happy to oblige.

One evening I received a short, emailed message from Sir Howard Fergus. "Surely," the message read, "by now, you should be able to publish a book of your poems." Sir Howard was always direct in expressing his thoughts, and I knew he was swinging a proverbial foot in the direction of my rear end. A book had, indeed, been in the mental works for years but needed that kick to move from thought to action. The editing process was tedious since there was not a definitive dictionary for the Montserratian language. In time, after several revisions, and with the invaluable help of some outstanding persons, in particular Chadd Cumberbatch, Edwin Martin, and Nerissa Golden, my first book, *Wha Marmie Say*, was published in January 2023, with a foreword by Sir Howard Fergus. I am forever grateful for his encouragement and inspiration. I thank God for His providential direction in the publication of that book, and for the positive reviews it has received.

The Montserratian cultural scene enabled me to blossom in other areas of service to the community. Involvement in the drama groups *Plenty Plenty Yac Ya-Ya* and the *Silk Cotton Theatre Group* developed a love for several elements of theatrical production. Dressmaking skills learned early at my grandmother's side, and further developed over many years, were put to good use in making costumes for a number of Masquerade troupes, as well as for other costumed groups in the festival parades, and for the Festival Queen pageants. There were other, more formal, opportunities for service, including stints on the Labour Advisory Board and the Public Service Commission.

Growing up in a service-oriented family and, in my teenage years, among a community of selfless and caring hospital staff, was to shape my perspective on contributing to my community. I saw in my first teachers - my grandparents and my mother - the lengths to which they would go to make life or situations better for others, sometimes for people they did not know, or who had not necessarily been as kind to them.

I saw dedication, loyalty, commitment, and occasions of sacrifice displayed by the nurses I grew up closest to, like Nurses Frances Ryan, Marjorie Joseph, Mary Cooper, Mary Mason and Catherine Barzey, among so many others. I saw it in several church and community leaders. I saw it in my own sister, who, just a few weeks before her death, left her own sick bed to go to help a friend who had fallen ill at night. And from them all I learned the adage that if something was worth doing, it was worth doing well.

Service meant fulfilling commitments I had undertaken, and doing them to the best of my ability, not for reward or even for praise, but just to know that I had contributed to the upliftment of my group, organisation, school, students, community or country.

That I received recognition for my service was heart-warming. Just knowing that someone in the local community considered me to be deserving of an award was humbling and deeply appreciated. However, in my mind, this was not to be flaunted, for "*exaltation comes neither from the east nor from the west nor from the south. But God is the Judge*" (Psalm 75:6-7a, NKJV).

Pride, I knew, was a dangerous trait, and I could not let it make a home within my heart or mind. I recognised that any success I had, any promotion, any award, comes from God who can both exalt and put down. Furthermore, it was even more humbling to realise that any human ability or habit or work that might have contributed to my success were gifts from God, and therefore, praise, honour, gratitude and glory were to be attributed to Him and Him alone.

Montserrat has been good to me. I believe this island is where I was Divinely appointed to be, despite birth in another country, and periods of living abroad. When it was time, I knew where home was. I joyfully cherish opportunities to give back to this land and its people – my people! And if it is God's will, Montserrat will remain home to me until I am called to "a better country" whose designer and builder is God (Hebrews 11:10,16 ESV).

CHAPTER NINE

The Gift of Music

If teaching has been one of the pivotal points of my life, music has been the other one. Since childhood, I had known of relatives who were established and reputable piano teachers, classical pianists and choral arrangers in New York. My maternal grand-aunt, Marie Evelyn Margetson (1890 – 1986) was a music teacher in Harlem, New York City for many years. Her brother, my grand-uncle, Edward "Teddy" Margetson (1891 – 1962) migrated to the US in 1919 and served as organist and choirmaster of the Church of the Crucifixion, also in Harlem. He founded the renowned Schubert Music Society of New York in 1927. He was a distinguished composer, particularly of choral music, and several of his compositions are located at the Rare Book and Manuscript Library at Columbia University in New York City.

My other maternal grand-uncle, Karl Margetson (1896 – 1983) had also migrated to New York and had a career in music teaching. He returned to the Caribbean and settled with his brother, my grandfather, in Montserrat in the 1920s. There, he excelled as a music teacher, composer, and organist at the St Anthony's Anglican church, until his death. Their father, my great grandfather John Henry Margetson, had served as choir director at the Bethel Moravian Church in Parsons, St Kitts, and their mother, Marie, has been described in a St Kitts historical document as "the finest pianist of her time."[13]

Apart from hearing my grandfather's baritone voice singing the hymns at church and singing funny songs with Beverley and me around the dining table as we awaited the serving of meals, I have no recollection of him displaying any distinctive musical talent which may have been passed down to him. Noel James Linnington Margetson had his own niche as a physician and surgeon. Nevertheless, he married a lady with distinctive musical genes. I mentioned before that my maternal grandmother, Clara Adelaide Steele Margetson (Nanny), had been a contralto singer in New York City.

It was my grandmother, Nanny, who insisted that Beverley and I take piano lessons. I cannot recall that we had any choice in the matter. At that time, we lived across the street from a piano teacher, Mrs Gladys Lewis, and we joined her class. Nanny and Grandad bought a piano, and Beverley and I attended music lessons consistently, but practising was more of a chore.

Whenever our grand-aunt Evelyn visited from New York, she supplemented our music lessons. These included exercises to harden our fingertips by repeatedly pounding each one against a wooden surface for a few seconds. It was very uncomfortable, and Beverley and I thought of it as a "New York drill" since it was only Aunt Evelyn who insisted that we do this. Once she returned to New York after her annual vacations in Antigua, Beverley and I happily abandoned the fingertip drill.

With Mrs Lewis as our patient and skilled piano teacher, we easily completed the introductory piano book and began the Grade One course, where we started learning to play with both hands at the same time. We were halfway through that book when Beverley and I went to live with Mummy in Montserrat. Unfortunately, my grand-uncle Karl Margetson had by then acquired a full piano teaching load, in addition to his duties as organist at the St Anthony's Anglican church. So, he reluctantly advised Mummy that he simply could not squeeze us into his schedule. I later learned that there were other music teachers on the island, but for some reason, Mummy did not apply to anyone else. Neither Beverley nor I had any more formal music lessons after moving to Montserrat. We did not have a piano at home in Montserrat, but there was a piano at school on which some friends taught us how to play *Chopsticks*.

It was around this time that an interest in playing a musical instrument was re-ignited. An opportunity was divinely provided, when my faith in Christ began to blossom at the Bethany Pentecostal Church in Plymouth, Montserrat. One day, the pastor's wife, Sister Howes, brought a piano accordion to church. I had never seen such an instrument before and found it extremely interesting. I was allowed to try playing it, and once I had got past the bulkiness and the need to keep the bellows continuously expanded and contracted by moving the right side of the instrument, I soon got the knack for it.

I cannot explain how or why, but soon, I was able to find the right keys to play the melodic line, and the right buttons to play the bass and accompaniment chords. I knew nothing about chord progressions or triads or anything like that. But I soon learned the basics, practically if not theoretically, and was able to accompany songs at youth meetings. Although I knew musical keys, notes, and rhythm, I was learning to play by ear. It was exhilarating.

When I asked and was allowed to borrow the accordion to practise at home, this further enhanced my budding interest, and I learned to hear intervals and chord changes. And as I heard the intervals and chord changes in my head, after a while, my fingers moved to play the notes and chords I heard. I had no one to teach me the techniques of piano accordion playing, and the modern opportunity to learn via the Internet did not exist in those days of the late 1960s in Montserrat. But over time, I gained more confidence in playing the piano accordion, albeit at an amateurish level.

It was at Erdiston Teachers' Training College in Barbados, the result of Divine intervention in my career plans, that I began the progression from piano accordion to piano and organ. In the main assembly hall at Erdiston stood a piano which was mostly untouched, except for periodic singing classes. As a boarding student, I was able to go to the assembly hall after classes were done for the day. The thought struck me that I should be able to transfer the basic chords and patterns which I had learned on the accordion, onto the piano. I had, by then, learned the major chord changes for a few keys - F, C, G, D and A.

One evening, I headed for the assembly hall, and started to play some hymns and songs. As I tried to transfer my knowledge and found that the transfer worked, I became increasingly enthusiastic. With no one around to disturb my practice, I was able very quickly to convert to piano playing. The basic piano lessons I had taken with Mrs Lewis in Antigua came back to help me. Notation, rhythm, and timing. I quickly became adept at playing basic tunes and harmonies by ear.

I had joined a church – The People's Cathedral - while at Erdiston College, and became actively involved in the choir. Once I became more confident in playing by ear, I asked the church organist whether I could practise playing the organ and was delighted when she agreed. Over the two years spent at Erdiston, I developed my playing technique rapidly, including learning to play the bass pedals on the organ. As I progressed, and as my college schedule permitted, I occasionally accompanied the Thursday morning Miracle services at church. This helped me to develop confidence and skill. Despite the lack of formal music lessons beyond the rudimentary first steps, God had plans I could not have foreseen until He was ready to put them into operation.

But that was not all. A few years later, when I began my undergraduate studies at the Cave Hill campus of the University of the West Indies, I was fortunate to find on-campus lodging. This allowed me to befriend other students who were not in my faculty, but who also resided on the hall of residence. One of these, a Trinidadian law student whom we called Joe, would often bring a guitar with him to play tunes while chilling on the expansive steps outside the hall in the evenings. As I sat outside the hall enjoying the cool breezes and the camaraderie of other students after classes, and listening to Joe playing the guitar, my interest in the guitar was peaked. By then, I had become a confident piano player and was curious to see how chords were formed on the guitar.

Joe was happy to oblige, passed over his guitar, and over a few days, taught me to play John Denver's popular song *My Sweet Lady* in the key of D. He also taught me a few other chord patterns on the guitar. I was delighted. When I was able to, I purchased a basic acoustic classical guitar, and with the help of a beginner's guitar chord book, I taught myself how to play some chord progressions on the guitar. Over time and with plenty of practice, I gained confidence and even periodically accompanied the singing at small group religious services held on campus.

I was about eleven years old when I became seriously interested in choral singing. The Christmas before we permanently moved to Montserrat, Beverley and I were spending the holidays with Mummy. As usual, we attended the traditional Christmas open-air event around the War Memorial in Plymouth, where various church and community choirs gathered in the square to sing carols. This year, the Montserrat Secondary School's Glee Club, under the direction of teacher and musical director Mr Stephen Adolphus presented the *Hallelujah Chorus* from Handel's "Messiah".

As the choir of teenagers burst gloriously into this rousing piece, I, along with others who were standing around, moved closer to gain a better vantage point to see this outstanding performance. It was truly unforgettable. For a pre-teen like me, it was hugely inspiring. Beverley and I were going to be attending the Montserrat Secondary School in the next school year, and I was definitely going to join the Glee Club.

By September 1964, when I entered the Montserrat Secondary School, Mr Adolphus was no longer teaching at the school. The Glee Club was being conducted by another teacher with a lovely personality, but whose style of choir directing was not particularly motivating. Yet, I really liked choral singing, and regularly attended the choir rehearsals which were held on Monday afternoons after school.

And then, a new teacher arrived at the school – a tall, elegant lady, who strode into the auditorium at rehearsal time one afternoon and became our new Glee Club Director. Her name was Edith Bellot Allen. And she forever changed the trajectory of my life as a singer. She was sharp and precise. She knew exactly the sound she wanted the choir to produce. And she knew exactly how to get what she wanted.

"The backs of chairs are for decoration," she insisted. "Sit forward and straighten your backs. Plant your feet on the floor so you can rise to your feet in one smooth movement."

"Drop your jaws and not your drawers," she would regularly chant. (She used every opportunity to give young ladies a mantra for good moral values). "Keep your knees together when you are sitting down."

Discipline became the cornerstone of the choir's success, and we students took the discipline to heart. We corrected any lapses in ourselves and in each other. Musical scales and vocal warm-ups became interesting and purposeful, and the repertoire of the choir widened to embrace a range of musical genres. One of the favourite pieces we learned was Johann Strauss' "*By the Beautiful Blue Danube*," which we performed at the school's graduation ceremony one year. Under Edith Bellot Allen's direction, the rehearsals were so enjoyable; I could not wait for Monday afternoons to get singing. Only later did I realise how much of our director's technique for teaching and obtaining good tonal control, proper enunciation, clear choral diction, proper breathing, and expanded vocal range, I had learned.

When I entered the University of the West Indies (UWI) at Cave Hill, Barbados, I discovered that Edith Bellot Allen was also there in her final year of studies. And she was the director of the campus choir, the *Cavite Chorale*. I was delighted and wasted no time joining the chorale. Our director had not changed. Her techniques were as strong and successful as I knew them to be. The membership of the choir included several incredibly talented singers from the region who were also studying at Cave Hill. Regular concerts were sold out, and the chorale's performances at campus graduation ceremonies were stellar. There was so much to learn from Edith's style of conducting and repertoire-building. Under her direction, musical repertoire and arrangements were diverse, including classical, sacred, modern, popular, and folk songs that appealed to a wide cross section of the community.

When Edith graduated, she passed the baton of leadership of the *Cavite Chorale* to me, and I accepted with deep humility and honour. While hers were large shoes to fill, she had prepared me well, simply by sharing her skill, knowledge, and high standards of choral excellence and discipline with us all. Effectively, Divine Providence had allowed my path to cross with hers in a way which ensured that I gained a wealth of knowledge and practical skills in choral conducting and arranging. She had become my mentor and friend. The next year that I spent directing the *Cavite Chorale* until my own graduation, was quite a productive one, both for me as a choral director, and for the chorale itself.

When I returned to Montserrat after graduation in 1977, Edith was there, directing the *Emerald Community Singers* (ECS), a local choir which had been founded about six years before. I joined the choir at her invitation, and once again was blessed to be sitting under the tutelage of such an inspiring and passionate choral director.

One of the highlights of my musical journey with the ECS was being part of the official Montserrat contingent to the 1979 Caribbean Festival of the Arts (CARIFESTA) in Cuba. We travelled to Cuba by ship, along with contingents from Antigua and St Kitts, and were entertained daily by the rehearsals of these groups. In Cuba, the ECS performed at various events, including as back-up singers for Montserratian soca legend Alphonsus "Arrow" Cassell, who was one of the headline acts for the festival.

I was a member of the Emerald Community Singers until I migrated to London in August 1980. By the time I returned to Montserrat in 1991, Edith had returned to her native land of Dominica and had assumed duties as the resident representative of the University of the West Indies on that island.

In 1988, while I was residing in the UK, a new choir was established in Montserrat by outstanding Antiguan musician Mrs Veronica Dyde together with Mrs Candia Williams, a close friend of mine. My sister Beverley had joined this choir, named *VOICES.* Under Mrs Dyde's skilful direction, the choir was soaring in reputation and repertoire. When I visited Montserrat on holiday in 1989, *VOICES* was preparing to stage a Christmas recital, and I was invited to join the choir for this production, which I did. I thoroughly enjoyed the experience. Two years later, when I returned to Montserrat permanently, I was asked to become the musical director of *VOICES* as Mrs Dyde had by then left the island. The accumulated training and experience which had been given to me over several years of association with Edith Bellot Allen and the choirs she had led, now provided me with the confidence to take on this new challenge. I directed the choral group *VOICES* from September 1991 until March 2010.

My path was to cross providentially with other choral leaders of international renown. These interactions helped to hone the skills I had learned from Edith and reinforced what she had taught me. I attended a concert in Antigua staged by the University Singers of the UWI Mona campus in Jamaica, conducted by Mr Noel Dexter, who was also the composer of a phenomenal array of both sacred and secular choral music. I asked the Montserratian resident representative of the University of the West Indies, Professor Sir Howard Fergus, to consider inviting Mr Dexter to come to Montserrat to conduct choral technique training. Sir Howard, always keen to promote cultural excellence, extended the invitation, and Mr Dexter travelled to Montserrat to conduct a choral workshop.

I benefitted enormously from this intervention. So too, did the choirs with which I worked at the time. Mr Dexter thrilled the participating choristers with his knowledge, skill, and the tangible results of his facilitation. He also generously held comprehensive discussions with me, in which he counselled me on aspects of choral theatre such as programme content and arrangement, choreography, attire, repertoire, and accompaniment. He later provided me with the scores of some Caribbean folk songs and spirituals which he had either composed or arranged and which the group enjoyed learning and singing.

The choral group *VOICES* soared beyond the shores of Montserrat. Performances in Antigua, St Kitts, and St Thomas built the confidence and performance expertise of the choir. In 2008, we were invited to represent the Open Campus of the University of the West Indies (the UWI) at the opening celebrations in Barbados to commemorate the 60th anniversary of the University. *VOICES* was part of a mass choir that featured the Cavite Chorale of the UWI at Cave Hill, Barbados, the University Singers of the UWI at Mona, Jamaica, and the Duke Ellington School of the Arts Chorus of Washington, USA.

VOICES also participated in the UWI's 60th anniversary Gala Concert at the Frank Collymore Hall in Barbados. In preparation for this concert, the group benefitted tremendously from the outstanding skills of world-renowned Jamaican choreographer Professor Rex Nettleford. He choreographed an entire Montserratian folk song for the *VOICES* performance and afterward sent a personal letter of commendation for the performance and potential of the choir.

Music continues to play a pivotal role in my life, and I am honoured and supremely blessed to be able to meet some of the musical needs at various venues. A few years ago, I attended an investiture ceremony for British awards at the Governor's Residence in Montserrat. As I arrived at the residence to take my seat among the other guests, an official approached me hurriedly. The ceremony was about to start, and the compact disc player from which the British National Anthem was to be played, was suddenly malfunctioning. Would I be able to play the National Anthem on the piano? There was no written score for the anthem available at such short notice, but I was able to play it perfectly by ear, which I did. The official who oversaw those arrangements was visibly relieved and thanked me profusely afterward.

I continue to direct the chorale at my local church and facilitate choral workshops in both vocal technique and repertoire for other choirs in Montserrat and overseas. I also regularly provide piano and organ accompaniment for worship services and other events in churches of various Christian denominations.

There is an unshakeable conviction that music has become such a strong component of my life and work, through Divine Providence. How else can I explain my ability to play musical instruments, to hear harmonies clearly, and to translate them to my fingers or into choral arrangements? How else can I explain the ways in which I have crossed paths with knowledgeable, passionate, and kind persons who have all so generously and patiently shared their expertise. As a result, despite very rudimentary formal musical training, I have been fortunate enough to make impactful contributions to musical enrichment of congregations and choirs at home and abroad.

These reflections never fail to lead me to humble thankfulness, for my journey in music continues, and my passion is undimmed. Music has added immense joy and depth to my life. May I never take this gift for granted nor smother it with pride. With the most profound gratitude and praise, I give all the honour and glory to God.

CHAPTER TEN

Careless Moments

We live in a world where crime abounds, man-made machines fail, and memory lapses occur. We cannot be too careful; whether we live in bustling inner-city London or a tropical paradise like Montserrat. I like to think I am mindful, but I know it is a trait I am still developing.

My reflections led me back to the end of March 1985. I had lived in London for almost five years and had not returned to Montserrat, even on vacation, during that time. Having settled into my new job and taken out a mortgage to purchase a small leasehold apartment, I could not have afforded to travel home to the Caribbean until now. My only sibling, Beverley, had just given birth to a baby boy. I was ecstatic. The past five years had been the longest period of separation in our lives. So, I scrimped and saved to finance a vacation trip to see my sister and meet my newborn nephew.

I had arranged for the purchase of my plane ticket through my aunt who lived in Montserrat. She had sent the plane ticket by registered mail, which I had collected from the post office earlier that morning. I was set to travel in two weeks and decided to go down to Oxford Street, a prime upscale shopping area of London, where one of the large department stores was having a sale. As I looked through the sale offerings, I picked up a few outfits to try on, but could not find anything I liked. I was reluctant to spend scarce funds on anything I did not like or need. So, I left the store empty-handed.

It was only when I had leisurely walked a block or more further along the street, window-gazing along the way, that it hit me that I was truly empty-handed. I did not have my handbag, which contained my bus travel pass, credit card, money, and my return plane ticket to Montserrat. Engulfed in a wave of panic, I flew down the street back to the department store I had just left, ran up the escalator, and charged my way to the last area of sale racks I had surveyed.

There was a chair against the wall close to the racks, and two salesclerks were standing over the chair, talking animatedly. On the chair, all alone, sat my handbag - in full view of anyone and everyone who had any interest in ladies' dresses on sale, or carelessly unattended bags.

"Excuse me," I said, with as even a tone as I could muster, given the wave of relief that had broken over me. A huge sigh escaped. "That's my handbag."

I reached out to take my bag from the chair, and one of the salesladies remarked that I was very lucky they had spotted it.

Although neither of them had shown any disbelief that the bag was indeed mine, on impulse I said, "I put it down to look at a dress and forgot to take it up. It has my airline ticket in it. I was so worried."

I quickly unzipped the bag, pulled out the ticket, and showed it to them. Thankfully, I also had picture ID documents in the handbag.

"Someone was watching over you," said one of the ladies. Indeed, Someone was. And He had even provided two guardian angels to walk around that area, notice the bag, and stand watch over it until I got back to the store to claim it.

There was another incident, chiselled into my mind, which occurred one afternoon around 1993 while I was driving in Dagenham, Montserrat. I was wearing a loose dress, and as I turned the steering wheel on a sharp corner, somehow the hem of the dress got caught in the gap where the steering wheel joins the top of the steering column. The steering wheel proceeded to spin, pulling my dress into the column, tightening it around my lower body, and making it impossible for me to steer the vehicle, or to control the grip on my clothes. I was quickly getting into a state of fright, but God had already got it all under control. The street was clear of all traffic, which was a blessing. As I had just slowed down to turn a sharp corner, the car was travelling at a moderate speed.

In Montserrat, we drive on the left. However, the steering wheel, uncontrollable under the circumstances, was veering the car to the right, the wrong side of the street. Had any other cars been travelling toward me at that time, there would most certainly have been a collision. I could no longer easily reach the brakes to stop the car, as the grip on my clothes impeded the effective movement of my lower limbs. And as God would have it (not luck!) – that section of the street was quite flat, not sloping downhill.

I knew next to nothing about troubleshooting cars but felt that I should attempt to run the car into the culvert on the right side, as this was the direction in which it was heading, and I was, at that stage, powerless to significantly change the trajectory. The culvert served as a shallow drain, and this proved to be the best course of action at that time. I did whatever limited manoeuvring I could, and the left front tyre hit the side of the culvert, causing the vehicle to stop. I applied the handbrake and killed the engine.

With my heart racing, I was, with some difficulty, able to slowly unwind my clothes from the steering column. I paused enough to thank God for deliverance in the situation, and to allow the effects of panic to dissipate from my mind and body. The vehicle was undamaged.

I am fortunate to have travelled quite widely, but find the actual journeying, whether by air or sea, tedious. One of my coping strategies is to travel light, avoiding both the inconvenience of hauling overweight suitcases, and the additional charges inflicted by airlines. I love shopping in the big cities to replenish wardrobe essentials, as well as for kitchen and household gadgets, useful stock for my sewing room, and helpful educational materials for school use in Montserrat. However, most of this is shipped home by sea, so my suitcase for air travel contains only the items that I need to have immediate access to.

After I had returned to live permanently in Montserrat, I continued to visit friends and family in London from time to time. I increasingly received requests to take a "little package" for others at my destination. After one or two incidents where the little package turned out to be a box of mangoes or a large (even if relatively light) item that could not fit either into my suitcase or handbag, I began to dread these requests. Saying "*No*" was a skill I needed to sharpen.

When I was about to return to Montserrat after a visit to London in the summer of 2013, I was asked by a friend to take a few items of clothing for his relative in Montserrat. I said that my suitcase was likely to be full and offered to send the clothing along with my items to be shipped. That was not possible, I was told, as they were needed more quickly. The evening before I was to travel, while I was out, the items were delivered to my accommodation - a tightly packed travel bag that could not fit into my suitcase but would have to be carried as additional luggage.

On arrival early the next morning at the airline's check-in desk at Victoria, in central London, I found that the cost to take the extra bag was prohibitive. I contacted my friend to come to the check-in desk to collect his bag, as I was unable to take it. I collected my travel documents from the airline clerk, having checked in my suitcase and obtained my boarding pass, and I sat to wait for my friend to arrive to take away his bag. He was quite apologetic, and we had a brief conversation. After saying goodbye, I gathered my handbags and boarded the non-stop train to London Gatwick Airport.

As the Gatwick Express whizzed along, passing beautiful gardens and row houses in turn, I thought I would fill some of the 30-minute journey by completing the travel form required for arrival into Antigua, my first destination. I reached into my handbag and discovered that my travel documents were missing. Despite frantic searching, there was no passport, no airline ticket, no boarding pass, and no travel form to be found. I distinctly remembered being handed the documents at the airline check-in desk at Victoria Station, so where were they?

With a deeply sinking realisation, it dawned on me with sharp clarity, that I had rested the documents on the ledge where I sat while putting down my friend's bag to await his collection. In the moments of relief when he arrived, and after handing him the bag and exchanging a few pleasantries, I had left the area without picking up my travel documents. Now I was already at least ten minutes into a thirty-minute ride on a non-stop train to Gatwick Airport. My flight would begin boarding in less than two hours.

My mental and emotional anguish was indescribable and mounted even further while trying to make frantic calls to the check-in station at Victoria. Eventually, a telephone number was answered, and a most pleasant individual patiently listened to my garbled story, and provided a response that was indisputably miraculous. A passer-by in the station at Victoria had spotted a set of documents on a ledge near the entrance, with no apparent owner nearby. Concerned that they may have been lost, the kind passer-by had taken the documents to the nearby airline check-in counter.

On examination of the boarding pass and passport, the clerk at the counter had recognised that the documents were genuine, and that the owner of the documents would be needing them to board a flight for which they had already checked in. The clerk, after consultation, had found another passenger headed for Gatwick who agreed to take the documents in a sealed envelope, and deliver them to the airline's flight desk at the airport. I was instructed to go straight to the flight desk on my arrival at Gatwick.

All I remember of the rest of the journey to Gatwick Airport is that it was spent in a mixture of self-recrimination over my carelessness, and the deepest, most heartfelt gratitude for the providence of God. He had, once again, lined up just the right persons to safeguard my property, make the right decisions about them, and bring them safely to me. I stepped off the train at Gatwick, found the airline's flight desk, and awaited the arrival of my documents. Half an hour later, the documents arrived intact and were handed to me upon confirmation of my identity.

How can I fail to offer all my praise and thanks to God for His providential care, even despite careless moments? Even then, He was thinking of me. His eyes were upon me, just as they are upon the sparrows. As He promised, "*...For I, the LORD your God, hold your right hand; it is I who say to you, "Fear not, I am the one who helps you*" (Isaiah 41:13 ESV). The brilliant hymn-writer, Fanny Crosby (1820 – 1915) penned these words under the pseudonym Victoria Stuart.[14]

In the shadow of the Highest
My defence shall ever be,
For His eye, that never sleepeth,
Still is watching over me.

What comfort, what hope, what assurance! Even in my careless moments.

CHAPTER ELEVEN

When 9 Becomes 6: Detours, Disappointments, and Death

If there is one certainty in life, it is that there will be disappointments. There will come those uncomfortably numbing experiences when hopes, dreams, and desires shrivel before our very eyes, and we feel that our hearts have been broken into a thousand pieces. What happened to the promise of Psalm 37:4 "*Delight yourself in the Lord, and he will give you the desires of your heart,*" we wonder, when our Cloud 9 expectations are upended, shattered, and become a rainy 6. Joy and peace fade, and are replaced by relentless aching and a gloomy outlook, sometimes bordering on depression. No rainbow appears in the sky. At least, that was my experience, until I realised that when the curtain was lifted, the breathtaking rainbow of Divine Providence always glowed brightly after the rain of disappointment and despondency. And always, there were tremendous lessons learned.

Growing up, like most girls I suppose, I dreamed of falling in love, getting married, and having children of my own. When my teenage aspiration for a career as a social worker was blown off course, I had no other career in mind. It was during this time that thoughts about my future became more centred around my childhood dream of getting married and raising a family. There was never one without the other. No baby carriage without prior marriage. Although others were doing it very happily – in fact, it was part of the culture I grew up with – I just could not picture voluntarily becoming a single parent to assuage my desire for children of my own. And in any case, this did not seem even a relevant consideration since, at the age of sixteen, I knew I was in love.

My high school sweetheart was a wonderful Christian young man, brought up in a devoutly Christian home, and he was the centre of my world. Our dates were always chaperoned. We either double-dated with other Christian young couples, or at my home or his home (both small houses) with our parents and siblings present. A great communicator, his intellect engaged mine with hours upon hours of deep discussion on a vast array of topics, and we grew closer as we explored our individual mindsets, plans, aspirations and goals, challenges, and troubles, over the years of our courtship.

A few years older than I, he graduated high school and went off to college overseas. Letters were sent and received, travelling by snail mail. There were no phone calls. There was no Internet, no email, no social media, or instant messaging service in those days. Long distance relationships really were long distance.

As time passed and I grew closer to adulthood, other interests occupied the empty time and space created by his departure. The doubts set in. Would he return? Was I really in love with him? Was he really in love with me? I was once again the unsure, unconfident, apprehensive young woman, contemplating an unsure future. I decided it was best to have certainty, and not to hold either my dearest or myself to a relationship which was in doubt, at least to me, at that time. So, I wrote, breaking off the relationship for the time being. It was a difficult letter to write, perhaps the hardest of my lifetime.

There was no response to my letter, no communication whatsoever, for around four or five months. Then I received a letter, which bore an extremely unusual harshness underlined with obvious hurt and anger. I bawled when I received it. Why had I not anticipated the anger? It appeared that while there were doubts on my end, there had been none on his. Thus, the contents of my letter struck him out of the blue.

This was confirmed a few months later when he came home for a short holiday. He visited me the evening of his return and told me how shattering my letter had been. I cried as he spoke, realising that I still loved him deeply, and that I had been mistaken in my doubts. He had dreamed of us marrying once he was done with his studies. He spoke gently, with no trace of bitterness, even though he was describing the mental, emotional, and almost physical shock my letter had brought him. In my heart, I had a growing sense of joy that he still loved me and that we would work it out with renewed understanding. My future was back on track – or so I thought.

The conversation lasted quite a while, and it was getting late. As he stood to leave, he turned to face me and told me that he had just got engaged to someone else. His fiancée was a college friend who had reached out to him when he was struggling with the pain and disappointment he felt after receiving my letter. He had found it easy to talk to her, and over the ensuing months, they had fallen in love. I was crushed; had not seen that coming. I wished him well. He returned overseas and married shortly afterward. News of his passing in late 2023 was deeply saddening. We had remained friends over the decades, although, at the time of his death, I had not seen him for over forty-five years.

I have struggled to understand why I had these needless doubts. Over the years, the *what-if's* have surfaced so many times until I learned to live in the present, mentally and emotionally. This did not come easily. It took years of self-discovery, prayer, and of realising that with God, I could excel in a life of singleness and offer myself in service to my community. This I have done with exceeding joy and energy, honing several skills along the way which, through God's grace, enhanced my capacity to serve.

Did I upend God's plan for my life when I wrote that impactful and fateful letter, breaking off a loving and meaningful relationship with a man who truly seemed God-sent? Did I set askew the Divinely appointed path for my future? I have learned from this experience, and many others, that life seldom follows our rules, and that our way is not always God's way, no matter how perfect it seems to us. There will be detours and disappointments as we find our paths on life's journey, and where our hearts and emotions are involved, these can be painful.

But I believe, on the strength of God's Word, that none of these detours and disappointments came as a surprise to God. Rather, they were signalling that God had other plans for my life, and the challenges strengthened me mentally and emotionally to embrace the Master's way. There were, however, periods when a life of singleness brought fresh emotional confusion and distress. Living alone in London raised feelings of loneliness which were hard to ignore. Working with families in my main job, and with children in my secondary work, it was easy to lapse into daydreaming about *what if...?*

I loved children – loved seeing them develop mentally, emotionally, and intellectually; loved answering their many questions. I loved taking care of them, as I did in my secondary work at the children's residential facilities in London. I took them on Saturday and Sunday outings to the park or to watch the jugglers and entertainers at London's famous Covent Garden. I took them for rides on the trains and other forms of amusement, entertainment, and activities planned by the residential care managers and staff. Frequently, I cooked and served tasty Caribbean foods that they enjoyed, and I played games with them. Occasionally, I took them to school and picked them up after school. Those were the happy, fulfilling times.

However, there were other experiences. Riding the buses, I would see women come aboard with babies or small children, and my eyes would well up with tears. Had my dreams of having a family of my own been derailed forever? Why, over the years, had I not been able to attract a life partner? Was I unattractive, too educated, unsociable? What made it worse were the too-frequent comments of others – male and female –

that so many men found me romantically attractive, therefore my singleness was because I did not want a man in my life. Really, I wondered? Where were these romantically attracted men?

Also hard to take were those people (especially the one or two who professed to be Christians) who admonished me that I was "wasting it." Several people strongly advised that I should at least "make a baby." My response that I did not want to have a child without being married was usually met with surprise that I would link children with marriage, as if one was a requirement for the other. I got laughed at.

It seemed like the last straw when, shortly after returning to live in Montserrat, I was found to have large fibroids, and following months of great discomfort and pain, a hysterectomy was recommended. But by this time, God had given me peace about childlessness. It happened at the right time. My mind and my heart were accepting. The news did not floor me. The only anxiety I felt was after hearing stories from other women who had had similar surgeries and had experienced hormonal issues afterward.

Some people advised me to go to England to have the surgery done. But I knew the doctors who would be giving the anaesthetic and performing the surgery, and I had complete faith in their skills. I elected to have the surgery performed in Montserrat. Much prayer was made, and the operation was successful. I healed quickly and did not experience any of the hormonal issues that others had warned me about. But any hope of having biological children was now extinguished.

Subsequently, I struggled with the new stark reality. A wave of spiritual warfare was on the rise, with an emphasis on the idea of supernatural breakthroughs and supernatural deliverance. After all, Psalm 37:4-5 tells us to "*Delight yourself also in the Lord, and He shall give you the desires of your heart. Commit your way to the Lord, trust also in Him, and He shall bring it to pass*" (NKJV). The all-seeing and all-knowing God knew the desire of my heart. I was a believer. Wasn't this promise for me, too? Why couldn't I simply "name it and claim it"? What was I missing?

I studied this verse, using context and commentaries, and eventually, the Holy Spirit shone a bright light of clarity on it. That is a story in itself, but the short version is this: I had to recognise that this was not a promise that God would simply give me whatever I wanted if I was good – that if I served God diligently, life would turn out just as I wanted it. Not at all. That was a sobering realisation. I had to see the verse in its context - that even when things were not turning out the way I desired, God was Sovereign. Trusting God was accepting that He was, and still is, in control, and that His will is perfect. And if I trusted him even when life was not turning out the way I wished it to, life would be truly satisfying. It was not about instant gratification.

I grappled with the truth that just because I desired marriage and a family did not mean that God was under any obligation to grant this. I might *think* that achieving my desires would lead to true fulfilment and happiness. But it was only a life of devotion to God - *delight in God* - that would bring true joy and satisfaction. I realised that my utmost joy and desire must rest in God, in His Word, in His service, before anything else. Matthew 6:33 echoes this same principle – "*But seek first the kingdom of God and his righteousness, and all these things will be added to you*" (ESV).

Again, I examined my "all these things," and they seemed good and worthwhile "things." I had to rest my faith in God who could see situations and circumstances I could not see. The transformation was not swift, but gradual. It took years for me to realise that delighting in the Lord was a process. It involved aligning my desires with God's desires, so that in the end, God's desires for me became my desires for myself. And because God's plans are better, I was able to find true happiness and fulfilment in my life.

What a life lesson I learned as I submitted my heart to God, and my desires to His will. And in the process, I discovered that singleness is a meaningful way of life and could also be a richly rewarding part of God's plan for my life. If I were destined by the Sovereign God to live in singleness, I would enjoy it, thrive in it, count my blessings and live in gratitude every single day. My relationship status did not define me.

God, in his Providence, brought me to a place of reconciliation between my hopes, dreams and desires, and His plan for my life. Through my career in teaching (into which He had ordered my steps), I have helped to mould and impact hundreds of children and young people at all stages, from nursery to college level. God has led me to successfully run a Girl Guide unit, teach hundreds of children the joy of scientific discovery through stimulating science projects, and help countless young children develop creative skills through introduction to computer technology.

In addition, there have been opportunities to coach scores of young people in developing debate speeches and public speaking skills. Doors have been opened for me to motivate multiplied cohorts of young adults through applied training in work and personal ethics, customer service delivery, principles of time management, and team-building. Through college-level and community-based discussions and research opportunities, I have been permitted to assist in building cultural awareness and national pride. It is a humbling realisation that despite my biological childlessness, I have been enabled to contribute to raising generations of children in Montserrat and abroad. God had plans for my life.

While God was dealing with me about my long-term life goals, I still had challenges dealing with short-term, spontaneous episodes of disappointment. Sometimes I would charge headlong, without due self-control, into verbal aggression. At other times, I would shrivel, shedding buckets of tears in self-pity, and hide myself away from the world. I would be impatient with delays and detours in achieving my ambitions and compare myself with others who appeared to have so effortlessly achieved theirs. On a few occasions, I would pretend that everything was fine, and try to dismiss how I was feeling when in the company of others. This was my modus operandi in the aftermath of disappointing outcomes, until I learned to handle day-to-day life more productively.

The result of this was that I was unhappy a lot, despite my love for the Lord. I wanted my plans for my life to be played out as and when and how I had planned. I was still learning to trust His way. I must have grieved the Lord in copious ways as I struggled to handle the vicissitudes of life. But again, He providentially took me through each bitter experience, and brought me out to the light of day, renewing my strength, and teaching me valuable lessons along the way. It is in these lessons that I grew both in faith, and in coping skills, and took positive steps towards developing emotional intelligence for negotiating life.

For instance, situations in which I felt that I was being treated unfairly, would often spark a confrontation. I would get very angry and found it difficult to control my emotions. One such incident occurred while working in London, as a senior employee in a small company office. I wished to take some vacation and travel back to Montserrat to see my family, whom I had not seen for a few years. Well in advance of the planned vacation, I requested leave for a period of six weeks to include the less busy Christmas and New Year period.

The Manager of the local office rejected my request, reasoning that this was too long a period of absence, given the small staffing complement, and the need to find a replacement for such an extended period. In addition, I only had five weeks' vacation per year, and so I would be borrowing one week's vacation from the next year, a period which had not yet commenced. I was livid. In hindsight, unreasonably so. In my utter disappointment, I did not think about my response. Rather, I got upset. Very upset. And I had a shouting match with the Manager of the unit. Of course, this did not resolve the matter at all, and only led to a decidedly cool atmosphere in the office, as the Manager and I avoided each other for the rest of the day.

I had been in similar situations before, where I vented my anger over disappointment in outbursts. I needed to learn self-control. That day, a powerful realisation struck me. How could I manage other people if I could not manage MYSELF? As a senior officer in the organisation, I was looked up to by other staff. I was even looked up to by managers and staff at other branches of the company, as well as at the Head Office. My attitude and behaviour were poor, especially in handling spontaneous disappointments, and would be a barrier to building strong and healthy collegial relationships, as well as to earning the respect of others.

In this instance, I had considered only my own desires without matching these to the needs of my work team. It was a difficult period of reflection, but I could not shake the feeling of sinfulness on my part. I knew that I had to climb down off my high horse and eat some humble pie. And I could not put it off. I had to act immediately.

I went to the Manager of my office, whom I had offended, and asked to speak with her. She coolly invited me in. I had struggled over what to say but knew I had to apologise. I could not apologise for requesting the vacation. Nothing wrong there. But I was wrong to have shouted at her, being disrespectful. I could have patiently listened to her explanation, calmly thought about it, and even taken a day or two to seek advice from the regional supervisory officer.

I faced the Manager and offered a profuse and sincere apology for being disrespectful and raising my voice to her. She graciously accepted my apology and to my utter surprise, told me that she also needed to apologise for the argument. In that instant, the ice was broken, and equilibrium restored. I left her office without a resolution but with a sense of restoration and peace.

Over the next few weeks, I approached the regional supervisory officer and asked whether there might be a way to resolve the situation, even if it meant reducing the leave requested by a few days. Over amicable negotiations, it was agreed that the vacation be granted, and arrangements were made to cover my duties. It might seem strange, but I did not feel that I had won. Rather, there was the realisation that I had exchanged my boxing gloves for a chair at the negotiating table. I had grown up, instead of acting like a spoiled child.

I am in no doubt that God providentially used this situation to teach me some valuable lessons. One of the most important was that disrespect to anyone at all was not an approach befitting a child of God, and that whenever I offended someone without proper cause, I needed to be the first to apologise. The constant impression I had during this incident was to "find something to apologise for. You could not have been 100% right in all respects, otherwise why do you have this feeling of having sinned in your anger?"

Another lesson, just as important, was that I could not allow other people to press my buttons or, as a good friend once told me, "Don't give away your power." After this, I became more aware of how I was dealing with instances of disappointment, delays, or detours in my life. I learned to assess the importance of each situation and to take some space for thought and reflection, before deciding on a course of responsible and appropriate action. I could have lost my job, but through God's grace and mercy, I did not. This has served me well.

I was, however, a work in progress, and some other notable occasions showed that I still had much to learn. Often I found disappointment happened because I did not communicate properly. The gap between what I thought I communicated and what the receiver of that communication actually received was sometimes too wide for a safe crossing. This lesson was one I have never forgotten.

I had a treasured friend who had been so kind to me. I wanted to show my appreciation, and during a conversation a few days before his birthday, I suggested that he pass by after work, on his birthday. He would drop by on occasion for a drink and a chat, so the invitation was not unusual by any means. He had a well-rounded theological perspective, and our chats were always welcomed and profitable. I planned to prepare a lovely meal for him.

That afternoon, I spent hours in the kitchen cooking. His workday ended at 6.00 p.m., and so I ensured that the meal was ready for his arrival, which I estimated would be around 6.30 p.m. I set the table beautifully, tidied the kitchen, and sat to await my friend's arrival. I had a specially chosen birthday card with sentiments that I hoped would express my heartfelt gratitude for his kindness to me.

6.30 p.m. came and went. So did 7.00 p.m. As did 7.30 p.m. and 8.00 pm. This was a few years before the widespread use of personal cell phones, and I could not reach him to ensure he was all right. At 9.00 p.m., when my guest had not arrived, anxiety about his well-being was replaced by annoyance that he had not turned up after all my labour in the kitchen. I had gone to all this trouble; I had not eaten so that I would be able to join him in this delicious meal that I had spent so much time and effort preparing.

Resentment crept up and threatened to stifle me. With a palpable sting of disappointment and anger, I sat down to eat alone, and then I cleared the table and put away the remaining food in the refrigerator.

I saw my friend a few days later, and I really tore into him. Why had he not contacted me to let me know he could not pass by for dinner on his birthday? I had spent so much time preparing a lovely meal, and I had waited and waited. I was really upset. He looked at me with a frown. He looked perplexed and concerned. I was not about to let him get away with his failure to show up. At last, with a look of bewilderment on his face, he spoke.

"But you never invited me for dinner!" he said.

It took a moment for that to sink in. And then it struck me! In my mind, my suggestion that he pass by after work was an invitation to relax and enjoy a meal. In his mind, it was a suggestion that, if time permitted, and he had no other plans, he could stop by and say hello. He did not usually have meals at my house, and as I had not mentioned dinner, he was completely unaware of my plans.

We were on two different wavelengths. I was operating on implication and assumption. He was no mind-reader. I had a lot to learn about clear and effective communication. It led to time-wasting and energy-sapping disappointment, and a rush to judgement because I had been put out. I had no one to blame but myself. It was a painful but important lesson. But God was shaping me for a life of service to my community, in which clear communication would prove to be a life-changing skill.

One of the greatest challenges in my faith journey towards understanding and embracing the Sovereignty of God in all of life's experiences, was coping with the loss of dearly loved ones. There were questions, apart from the fear of dying itself. Was the physical process of death painful? Would death be sudden or lingering? Would a diagnosis of a life-threatening illness curtail happiness and peace? In addition to these sorts of questions, there was also the grief and the painful period of trying to adjust to the tremendous loss.

I had had to deal with death since I was twelve years old, when my grandfather passed away. Over the next sixteen years, I lost other close relatives: my grandmother, two uncles, an aunt (who was brutally murdered), and both of my parents. As difficult as these were, I had tremendous support particularly from my sister Beverley, my only sibling and my best friend, and we comforted each other.

When Beverley was diagnosed with breast cancer at the age of forty-three, it ushered in a most distressing period for all of us. A pall also descended upon me – had God destined all my immediate family to shortened lifespans? After all, Daddy had died at forty-five, Mummy at fifty-six, and here was Beverley now fighting for her life aged only forty-three, with so much to live for. Her beloved son Kriston was eleven years old and about to begin secondary school.

One of the volcanoes in our homeland had started an eruptive phase the year before, causing severe upheaval to the entire population. With forced evacuations of our village, relocations, school disruptions, and a myriad of other inconveniences, it became too challenging for Beverley to remain in Montserrat. She needed a more settled environment and access to specialist medical care. She made the heart-wrenching but necessary decision to relocate to the United Kingdom. There, despite her unrelenting health condition, she embraced life in positive pursuits, growing both in her faith and in dedication to the preservation of Montserratian culture among other relocated persons.

Her death, four and a half years later, was the biggest blow I have ever had to bear. Born just one year and two weeks after me, she had always been there. It had always been "Ann Marie and Beverley". She died on the day after her son's sixteenth birthday. The week before her passing, Beverley confided to me that she had put her trust in Christ as her Saviour, believing fully in His atoning death. She had stepped up to the altar at church during the Sunday morning service, as a public declaration of her salvation through faith in Christ. The day after she did so, she was admitted to hospital.

Little did any of us realise that just six days later, she would be called home to Glory. The God of mercy and grace had been with her. What an inestimable comfort that was!

The day before the funeral, I went alone to the private viewing of her body. Looking at her lying lifeless, dressed beautifully in the light gold outfit which her best friend and I had selected, I voiced my heart's thoughts into the air around us. I reached out and gently stroked her arm. Her body was cold. More than twenty years later, that image remains vividly with me. And over and over, it reminds me of that powerful message from the apostle Paul:

> *...And you were dead in the trespasses and sins in which you once walked ... But God, being rich in mercy, because of the great love with which he loved us, even when we were dead in our trespasses, made us alive together with Christ—by grace you have been saved— and raised us up with him and seated us with him in the heavenly places in Christ Jesus, so that in the coming ages he might show the immeasurable riches of his grace in kindness toward us in Christ Jesus. For by grace*

> *you have been saved through faith. And this is not your own doing; it is the gift of God, not a result of works, so that no one may boast* (Ephesians 2:1-2; 4-9, ESV).

Here was God, illustrating an important scriptural truth to me in a way that would stay with me forever and cause me to give continual reflection and heartfelt praise. For the first time, I understood that I could never have come to faith in Christ unless God had first made me alive. Stroking my deceased sister's arm and speaking to her could not reach her, because she was physically dead. I now saw that in my state of spiritual death before conversion, no preaching, no human attempt at persuasion could have penetrated my heart and mind and led me to salvation had God not first made me spiritually alive to be able to receive the truth. And the same applied to Beverley as well as to all others who have been saved by grace.

How deeply this struck me. The implication of this real-life application of the scriptures pierced my soul and made me understand that I owed everything to God. I saw that it was *by grace* that I was saved – *it is the gift of God* – there was no work that I did. It was not because of my decision. I could boast of nothing. Even the very faith that I had in Christ's death and resurrection to effect my salvation was a gift from God. This was an awe-inspiring revelation. I am so grateful that God led me to understand and embrace this important and humbling truth.

There was a further profound lesson I learned through the distress of death. I have been particularly close to four of my cousins, all siblings, who grew up in nearby Antigua: Judy, twins Lesley and Keva, and their brother Robin. Keva and I shared a special bond through our efforts in cultural development – she in Antigua, and I in Montserrat. We shared ideas, strategies, and a deep desire for the preservation of the culture of our respective homelands, especially against the onslaught of cultural penetration particularly from the US.

Keva, seven years younger than I, had been the epitome of good health, high energy, and intellectual strength. She radiated sheer optimism, infectious enthusiasm, and boundless joy. She was also highly influential, in the most positive and productive way. So when Keva became ill in early 2008, at the age of forty-eight, and received a diagnosis of cancer, our shock was tremendous. This simply could not be happening. Not to Keva – one of the brightest lights of our family, and the life and soul of any gathering. Over the course of a few months, Keva fought for her life with all her might and never lost either her positivity or her joy.

I made the short air-hop over to Antigua to see her and was always amazed at the strength of spirit she possessed. Her faith was inspiring. One weekend in mid-November, 2008, I visited her. As I lay across one of the beds in her room, we shared our deepest reflections as we always did. One morning, she spoke of her faith in God and in His sovereign power over her life. She had been supremely blessed throughout her life, she said, and continued to be blessed each and every day.

"Annie," she said, with joy on her face and strength in her voice, "I wake up each morning, and wait, with great anticipation, to see what God is going to do today."

Those words stayed with me, and resonated deep in my spirit, even after I returned home.

I had promised to visit again two weeks later, in early December, but one week before that, I received a call from her twin, Lesley. She told me that Keva's condition had deteriorated, and she asked me to return to Antigua quickly. I did, and found Keva drifting in and out of consciousness. Other relatives came, and on Sunday evening, the last day of November 2008, we gathered around Keva's bedside and softly prayed and sang spirituals. A sense of peace pervaded the atmosphere. During that time of quiet reflection and prayer, Keva took her last breath and peacefully, victoriously crossed over her Jordan. The nurse checked her vital signs and tenderly whispered to us, "She's gone."

Being present with Keva just before and at the point of her death profoundly changed my apprehension about death. From being a scary prospect that I had always dreaded and honestly wished would never happen to me, I realised that in Christ, it was truly a crossing over into a new realm; one where there would be no pain, no sickness, only anticipation of endless joys. I was in awe. Once again, God had countered my fear of death with a beautiful example of the death of one of His saints, who died full of faith in the Lord.

Through these varied and providential experiences, I learned that I had no monopoly on crushed dreams and painful loss. Since the beginning of time, people had grappled with uncertainty, detours, disappointment and death. The Bible is replete with examples, and the experiences of saints such as Job, Joseph and Esther are profound. Furthermore, the book of Hebrews (Chapter 11) also lists a number of spiritual heroes like Abraham, Moses, David, and Sarah, who each made a choice to trust God through difficult situations which could otherwise have sapped their faith. They relied on the faithfulness of God and trusted in His loving providence.

I have learned that God has all the resources needed to carry me through every circumstance of life, and I can trust His plans for my future. I can rest in the assurance of Jesus who says:

> *Look at the birds of the air: they neither sow nor reap nor gather into barns, and yet your heavenly Father feeds them. Are you not of more value than they? ... Therefore, do not be anxious, saying, 'What shall we eat?' or 'What shall we drink?' or 'What shall we wear?' For the Gentiles seek after all these things, and your heavenly Father knows that you need them all* (Matthew 6:26, 28. 31-32, ESV).

My task is to serve Him with my whole heart right now, in the place where He has set me, whether that be in singleness, childlessness, through disappointment, devastating loss, unmet personal desires, or any other situation. I cannot be so distracted by life's challenges and disappointments, painful though they may be, that I fail to appreciate the amazing ways in which God is working out His purpose in my life. I have found the assurance which accords with Lamentations 3:32 – 33:

> *Though He causes grief,*
> *Yet He will show compassion*
> *According to the multitude of His mercies.*

For He does not afflict willingly,
nor grieve the children of men (NKJV).

With a renewed sense of awe and gratitude, I am learning to embrace and apply the lessons from each experience, and pray that in doing so, my life may honour Him.

CHAPTER TWELVE

Three Score and Ten

Birthdays have traditionally been high on the list of celebrations in my family. Starting with the early morning telephone calls from relatives and friends overseas, and now, in the Internet age, with social media posts beginning on the dot of midnight, birthday celebrants are truly celebrated. Having lost my parents and sister while they were still relatively young, it was a huge blessing to have attained the age of sixty-nine. I alone had been left standing. I was profoundly grateful to God, as I realised there was nothing I could have done to deserve a longer life than my loved ones.

So, with my seventieth birthday approaching, I dreamed of a significant celebration. Fine dining for my closest friends at a really nice restaurant or traveling to Antigua to celebrate with my dearly beloved family at the spectacular Shirley Heights' Sunday afternoon barbecue. As the date drew closer,

I decided on a Montserrat celebration for this special birthday, with plans for a post-birthday celebration in Antigua a few weeks later. After all, I reasoned, I would be seventy all year long, so I could celebrate all year long!

But God had other plans. On the morning of my seventieth birthday, the long dreamed-of, planned-for, and excitedly awaited threescore-and-ten of my existence, I woke up to the sound of nurses' trolleys being wheeled into my room at the Sir Lester Bird Medical Centre in Antigua. Two nurses began the early morning routine of monitoring vital signs - blood sugar and pressure, pulse rate, body temperature and oxygen saturation. So how had I got here?

Since the consultations at the Glendon Hospital in Montserrat with Dr. Myron Rolle and his US-based Caribbean Neurosurgery Foundation team (which I related in Chapter One), many wheels had turned behind the scenes. Most of these I only learned about later. The doctors had conferred and decided that I needed urgent surgery, but the hospital in Montserrat did not, at that time, have the necessary facilities for the recommended surgical procedure. Dr. Rolle and the surgeon in Montserrat, Dr. Kassim, had quickly arranged for me to be transferred to the hospital in Antigua, and to be accepted as an in-patient in the surgical unit.

The team of neurosurgeons who came to my bedside at the Glendon Hospital in Montserrat on Sunday April 3, 2022, continued to monitor my condition. They also collected samples of the dripping fluid from my nose for testing. They were due to be leaving Montserrat on Tuesday April 5, to begin their mission in Antigua. A few hours before the team's departure from Montserrat, Dr. Rolle came to my bedside along with Dr. Kassim, and they clearly set out the diagnosis of my condition and the recommended course of action. They explained that I would need to be transported to the hospital in Antigua and that the arrangements were being finalised. I was to leave the very next morning.

"We are going across to Antigua this afternoon," said Dr. Rolle, after the procedural details had been communicated. He gave me a look of reassurance and a gentle nod. "We will meet you there." I returned a weak smile, which I hoped conveyed thankfulness, rather than the fright I tried to mask.

"Thank you," was all I could say, in that overwhelming moment. The brief meeting was over. I sent up a prayer. Fervently, and silently.

"Lord, you know all about my condition. You sent this team from the US at just the right time. This was your plan to help me. Thank you, Lord. I am placing myself and all these arrangements in your hands. I ask that your will be done in this situation. Please help me to trust you, and calm my spirit."

If ever a time Psalm 57 has spoken to my soul, it is in recalling that moment. As verses 2 - 3 state: "*I cry out to God Most High, to God who will fulfil his purpose for me. He will send help from heaven to rescue me*" (NLT).

In the hospital, lying flat on my back for hours on end, I found tranquillity in prayer. Short prayers were breathed out to God in my thoughts and in whispers. I could not pray 'decree and declare' prayers for healing – somehow, it seemed inappropriate. The biblical injunction in Matthew 7:7 (NKJV) to "***Ask**, and it will be given to you; **seek**, and you will find; **knock**, and it will be opened to you*" spoke clearly to me. As did John 5:15 (NKJV) "*Now this is the confidence that we have* *in Him, that if we* ***ask*** *anything* ***according to His will****, He hears us.*" [Emphasis added]

My thoughts took me to the account of the Apostle Paul, burdened by the thorn in his flesh. He prayed. He pleaded with God. And God responded to his prayer by showing Paul that He had a plan even for this crisis. And I knew He had a plan for me too. I knew He would never leave me or forsake me. He promised in His Word. That I could declare with confidence, and in my situation, this was reassuring. So, I relied on Him. I yielded to His will. And in the midst of it all, I was strengthened and I had peace. Oh, I still had moments of nervousness, especially as I was in uncharted waters. I was particularly concerned about how I would meet the costs (as yet unknown, but expected to be substantial) of the hospitalisation and treatment in Antigua. But I knew that God was able to carry me through, meet my needs, and give me the endurance to bear whatever came, just as He had done for the Apostle Paul.

God also sent ministering angels. I found emotional support through the kindness, warm words of solace, and graciousness of the nursing staff at the hospital in Montserrat, which I greatly needed at that time. The small team of nurses was stretched thin, especially since most of the relief medical and nursing team from Cuba, who had been providing much needed staffing assistance during the COVID pandemic, had ended their stint just days before.

There were several patients hospitalised at that time too. The patience I saw exerted by each nurse over those days was nothing short of angelic. I do believe that God had indeed endued each of them with enabling grace that I had the privilege of witnessing personally in real time. And still, by

Divine Providence, they found the time, the energy, the grace, and the empathy, to speak words of peace and reassurance to my nervous heart.

Nurse Shaumen Gray was one of these nurses. A busy wife, and mother of active twin boys, she had nevertheless worked overtime to help cover staff shortages. Her shift was long over, but she came to my bedside to offer words of encouragement as I shared my nervousness.

"I understand how you are feeling," she said, "but don't worry. Everything is going to work out. You will be well taken care of. You will be fine."

Her tone was as no-nonsense and matter-of-fact as usual. That was expected. She had seen a lot of suffering, unexpected situations, and even death, in her career, and she was straightforward in her communications. But her eyes reflected a depth of compassion and her look was one of reassurance. A calmness came over me, and I knew God had just sent one of His angels to comfort me.

The next morning, Wednesday April 6, the day before my birthday, the ambulance arrived to drive me to the airport for the special medical evacuation flight that had been arranged to take me to Antigua. As I boarded the plane, one of my closest friends, who had come to see me off, shed tears.

"May God take you safely," she said. "I am praying for you."

"Thank you," I replied. "God bless you. Keep in touch."

I arrived safely in Antigua, where an ambulance whisked me to the Sir Lester Bird Medical Centre in the capital city, St Johns. My sister-cousin, Lesley, was also on hand to welcome me, staying with me for the first hour at the hospital to help me through the various procedures for admission. I was taken for diagnostic imaging CT scans and x-rays, before being wheeled to a comfortable room in the surgical unit.

There I spent the day before my birthday getting used to the surroundings, the nursing staff, and the hospital routine of periodic vital checks. Interspersed with these were the most welcomed visits from family members and a few Montserratian friends who lived in Antigua. They had heard that I was in hospital there and so they visited to express their well wishes and to offer tangible assistance if needed. The groundswell of support was unexpected and so heart-warming.

At around the same time, Dr. Patrick Knight, a consultant neurosurgeon based in Trinidad, was preparing to travel to Antigua. Antigua had no resident neurosurgeon. While the hospital there had more advanced facilities than the hospital in Montserrat, it lacked some of the equipment needed for the recommended procedure to correct my cranial defect. Dr. Knight visited Antigua periodically to provide neurosurgical consultancy. Dr. Rolle had made timely contact with him to join the Caribbean Neurosurgery Foundation (CNF) team in Antigua. He was to bring the necessary tools with him to carry out the first transnasal endoscopic cranial repair surgery to be performed in Antigua. I knew none of this until several weeks later.

My birthday dawned. It was a beautiful day. I could see the bright sunlight streaming in through the window in my spacious hospital room. Several text messages awaited my rising, most from persons who did not know that I was out of Montserrat, or in hospital. A beautiful bouquet of flowers arrived from family members with two huge balloons announcing that I had arrived at my seventieth birthday. I had visits from friends, including one who brought me a slice of home-made black fruit cake, which was my favourite dessert. At the doctor's rounds, a larger-than-usual contingent of doctors and nurses descended on my room singing the birthday song. It was a lovely gesture which I deeply appreciated.

In the late morning, the team of neurosurgeons came to see me and I was introduced to Dr. Knight from Trinidad. The surgeons explained the details of the operation which I was to undergo that same evening. They patiently listened to and answered my questions. As they were leaving, one of them cautioned me not to eat anything else before the surgery. I suddenly remembered the slice of cake that I had been looking forward to eating. But orders were orders. When my cousin Lesley visited me later that afternoon, I handed her the cake and asked her to take it to her home and refrigerate it for me. I made it clear that I wanted to eat my cake when I was able to have it!

In the evening, the orderlies arrived to take me to the operating theatre. I had had a good birthday so far, although not the way I had hoped or planned to celebrate it. There was one more outstanding and uplifting interaction which awaited me right outside the operating room, immediately before the surgery commenced. Dr. Butler and Dr. Rolle from the visiting neurosurgical team, Dr. Knight, consultant neurosurgeon, and the Anaesthetist, gathered around the gurney on which I lay waiting to be wheeled into the operating room. Each of the neurosurgeons spoke to me - briefly, simply, and clearly - once again establishing the diagnosis of my condition, and recapping the procedural steps ahead; gentle voices, confident in the approach being taken, and providing an oasis of calm and peace. The reassurance I felt was profound. I was truly in the hands of caring and capable professionals. Dr. Rolle tapped my right shoulder.

"I am so glad that we saw you in Montserrat and got you across to Antigua," he said. "We're going to take good care of you."

And they did.

I woke up from the three-hour-long surgery with my nostrils plugged and my entire nose completely bandaged shut. I could only breathe through my mouth. It was quite uncomfortable, but gloriously, the residual pain was not unbearable. I experienced mild aching in my sinuses, and in the stitched-up area of my right thigh which they had cut into and from which fatty tissue had been harvested to plug the leak in the dura inside my skull.

On April 7, 2022, my "three-score-and-ten", God gave me a wonderful birthday gift. He used a team of specialist surgeons who, like in the fairy tales of my childhood dreams, arrived out of nowhere without any inkling of mine, in the right place and at just the right time, to save my life. The co-ordination between medical personnel in distant places - Montserrat, the USA, Antigua, and Trinidad - was awe-inspiring on its own. Several months after this episode, I read and re-read Isaiah's account of God's supremacy over His creation:

> *I am God, and there is none like me. I make known the end from the beginning, from ancient times, what is still to come. I say, 'My purpose will stand, and I will do all that I please. From the east I summon a bird of prey; from a far-off land, a man to fulfil my purpose. What I have said, that I will*

> *bring about; what I have planned, that I will do* (Isaiah 46:9-11, ESV).

I must confess to having a little chuckle at verse 11. God did, indeed, bring men from far-off lands to fulfil His purpose in my life. Oh, the immense benefits of God's plans for His children. What an infinitely loving God we serve!

And so, I realised that my assignment on earth was not yet finished. However many more days, months or years that lay ahead for me, I still had a purpose (God's purpose) to fulfil. As I contemplated the future with this understanding, it struck me that God does not usually reveal His plan to us in advance. So, I needed to trust His will and His way. I needed to embrace the instruction and the reward of Proverbs 3:5-6 in its entirety: "*Trust in the LORD with all your heart, and lean not on your own understanding; In all your ways acknowledge Him, and He shall direct your paths*" (NKJV).

CHAPTER THIRTEEN

What Shall I Render?

Some years ago, one of my most treasured mentors lay terminally ill, and wished to speak with me. She had been such a blessing to me over several years as I sought her wise counsel, and she generously provided empowering advice with liberal doses of encouragement. When we spoke, her voice, although weakened, was clear. As always, strong diction and clarity were the hallmarks of her speech. Her last words to me that afternoon remain emblazoned across my heart and mind.

"I have enjoyed my life," she said, as we ended the short conversation.

Less than a week later, she took her last breath, and her earthly tenure was completed. A lifetime of service – most likely a combination of successes and failures, desires met and unmet, joy and sorrow, frustration and satisfaction – was at an end. She had been passionate about education, human resource management and choral music. We had so much in common. I knew, too, that hers was also a lifetime of thankfulness, gratitude to God, and joyful contentment. Since then, I have had many occasions to think of her, and of her assessment of her life.

Would this be my assessment of mine as well? The more I thought about it, the more I realised that my perspective on life and life's events, possibilities, and outcomes is circumscribed by my limited vision. I can see only what is directly in front of me. I do not have a long-range view of all the circumstances and situations which are likely to impact my life. But God has that long-range view, through which all the events of the universe and in the lives of His created beings are clearly seen from beginning to end (Isaiah 46:9-10).

Furthermore, God's omniscience makes His perspective more trustworthy, sharper, and complete. All of creation is in His hands. Therefore, even when life appears turbulent or mysterious or unreasonable, God is not perplexed. My mentor and friend had discovered this, and resting in the loving will of a gracious Heavenly Father, she was happy. In hindsight, I began to see that it was indeed possible to enjoy life, and to live with hope and joy, despite challenging circumstances.

When I began writing, it was to record my runny nose experience with as much detail as possible. I wanted to protect this momentous episode in my life, and its resolution, against the possibility of memory loss. I hoped that by God's grace, it would serve as a stimulus for the praise and glory that is surely due to Him.

But as I reflected on God's guidance in my life, on the many occasions in which challenges, pain and sorrow have beset me, and on cherished plans and dreams that have been turned upside down by an unseen hand, even my plan for this book changed.

With the benefit of hindsight, I began to take stock of the opened doors, lessons learned, intellectual, moral, and spiritual growth and development, and exciting new paths to follow which have come with each situation. Collectively, these experiences allowed me opportunities to serve God, my community and the upcoming generation in a variety of ways.

Why was I granted the joy and blessing of a hugely supportive and very loving family? Why was the door to a career in education suddenly opened? Why did my dream of marriage and motherhood remain unfulfilled? Why did my journey lead me to productive work and spiritual discovery in England? Why did it lead to other enormous and unforeseen benefits, some of which were not realised until more than two decades later at exactly the time they were needed?

Why was Montserrat selected as my country of abode for most of my life? Why did my dream of home ownership fall into place through a natural disaster? How, and why, did a hidden talent in music suddenly come alive with only rudimentary tutoring? Why did that team of neurosurgeons under the newly-established Caribbean Neurosurgery Foundation land on the shores of Montserrat, a neurosurgical wilderness, just when my life depended on their specialist skills? It was all to fulfil the purposes of God for my life.

However, looking back over three-score and ten years, I also saw that my life had not reflected the depth of gratitude for the blessings I had received and continue to receive through the providential hand of God. Each new day brought new benefits of His grace, new opportunities, and new commitments. God has been so faithful in keeping His promises; so good to me.

With stark honesty, I had to admit that my life had become crowded. So busy, so caught up in the hustle and bustle of my busyness, that I was not spending enough time with the God who had given me everything. I had allowed other pursuits to take over in my life. And still, God continued to pour blessings into my life. I needed to urgently reassess my priorities!

I had no claim to special privilege in blessings. Matthew 5:45 (NKJV) makes it clear that God "*makes his sun rise on the evil and on the good, and sends rain on the just and on the unjust.*" In other words, God is faithful, even when I am not. He blesses us even when we do not deserve the blessings. It was most humbling to learn that God's plan for my life did not depend on whether I had read my Bible diligently, prayed sufficiently, or had attended church faithfully. His plan is based upon His love for me, His purposes and intentions for my life, and upon how, when and where He plans to use my life to be of benefit to others for their good and His glory. What a generous, kind, loving God we serve!

In these reflections, I have traced the hand of Divine Providence in several ways, ordering and altering plans in my life. The benefits that have rebounded and the mercies shown to me are all of God's doing. The people through whom these benefits and mercies have been so gloriously poured out, have been instruments used by God to deliver His goodness to me. But the planning and the execution have all been the work of God, who deserves all the glory.

A scriptural adage, learned in childhood, centred itself in my mind. "*For everyone to whom much is given, from him much will be required; and to whom much has been committed, of him they will ask the more"* (Luke 12:48, NKJV). I have received bountifully from the Lord. In my reflections, I had to ask myself, along with the Psalmist, "*What shall I render to the Lord for all His benefits toward me?"*

The answer was, "I *will take up the cup of salvation, and call upon the name of the Lord"* (Psalms 116:12-13, NKJV). The Psalmist was alluding to the ancient custom whereby, at a celebratory feast following a great victory, the king would lift a cup of wine, and drink from it in thanksgiving for deliverance and victory. I needed to adopt the same attitude of gratitude, even though I could never render to God anything even remotely comparable to the benefits I have received. But I can, out of a heart of gratefulness, acknowledge His supremacy and sovereignty and lordship of my life, and I can embrace opportunities to share the good news about what He has done, with others.

That is the purpose of this book. It is not a chronological story of my life, but rather, a reflection on meaningful situations, events and circumstances that have built my faith in the sovereignty, love, faithfulness, goodness, and grace of God. Through these episodes, many of them serendipitous, even fortuitous, I have been able to trace a gracious Providence which has lit the path of my life. To have been shown this, in my lifetime, is an enormous blessing. I desire that the remainder of my life will be an offering of praise to God who has surrounded my life's journey with His mercy, grace, and kindness. I know that He who has planned my life in meticulous detail will continue to guide that plan to its final fulfilment.

As I have experienced, God's plans will not always correspond with our dreams, hopes and vision. The journey to the fulfilment of God's plans may lead through rocky roads and deep waters. It is sometimes difficult to have faith that the plan will work out for our ultimate good, when all we can see is the immediate disappointment of unfulfilled dreams, the crushing pain of loss of a dearly loved one, the anxiety of facing an uncertain future without the means to meet our needs, or the sudden onset of serious illness of ourselves or our loved ones. It can be hard to trust God when things just don't seem to be working the way we hoped, dreamed, or planned.

I had to learn that adverse circumstances and seemingly impossible situations neither take God by surprise, nor are beyond His capacity to handle or provide succour and strength. I also had to learn that there is no problem too small to merit His concern or His plan. And that His promise that He would *never leave us or forsake us* (Hebrews 13:5b, ESV) was unshakeable.

The great Christian evangelist, Charles Haddon Spurgeon, underscored this precious promise in an anointed message to readers of his daily devotional. His words have been such a blessing, especially when feelings of despair washed over me:

> *You may fear that the Lord has passed you by, but it is not so: He who counts the stars, and calls them by their names, is in no danger of forgetting His own children. He knows your case as thoroughly as if you were the only creature He ever made, or the only saint He ever loved. Approach Him and be at peace.*[15]

I have learned the essential nature of prayer; not just the formal schedule of a prayer time, but the need to continuously be in communication with God throughout the day. Prayer which acknowledges and submits our plans, hopes, desires and needs to his absolute sovereignty. My experiences confirmed what the Word of God had already told me, that He alone knows what is best for me. (Matthew 6:8; Luke 12:29-32). And our lives are in His hands, whether we have "given our lives to Him" or not.

I learned to draw from Jesus' example of prayer – *not my will, but Thine* – and to recognise that God's will must be paramount in all things. I had to choose between the desire for God's will to be done, and the desire for personal needs, and comfort. Even my own pride had to be surrendered to His will. I had to learn to give up my plans and exchange them for God's plans. But when I did so, I found a greater dimension of peace, comfort, contentment, and faith in His Sovereign power to work all things together for my good and for His glory.

My faith has increased exponentially. Many years ago, I prayed for the salvation of a friend, whose lifestyle was a source of distress to his loved ones. Knowing the personality of my friend and his casual attitude to God, it seemed that salvation was a long way down the line in a list of possible outcomes. Each time I prayed, the thought would enter my mind that this was a tough request. I would remind God that there was nothing impossible for Him to do, all the while also thinking "*Lord, I believe, help Thou my unbelief*" (Mark 9:24, KJV). Nevertheless, I continued to pray. Several months later, with immense joy, I received word that my friend had come to faith in the finished work of Christ at Calvary and had publicly confessed Christ as Lord and Saviour. There were confirming reports of the complete turnaround of his life and lifestyle. His conversion was a blessing and continues to be to this day.

As I recounted earlier in this book, when despair and anxiety drove me to my knees in my attempt to sell my apartment in London, I recalled the indescribable peace which flooded my soul as I turned the matter over to God for His will to be done. Episodes like these have boosted my belief in the power of prayer and of complete dependence on God working according to His will. When confronted with challenging situations, I return in hindsight to these experiences, and know that the God who lifted my burdens then, and who changed my friend's life, can do it again.

I have encountered an abundance of proof that God indeed orchestrates all things for good for those that are called according to His purpose. As my experiences show, "all things" include those situations that are bad, painful, and distressing. I have found that He will provide joy in sorrow, peace amid turmoil, hope in distress, and faith in times of fear and uncertainty. Every situation in the life of a believer will serve to accomplish His Divine purpose.

Indeed, each experience of Divine Providence in my life has renewed my confidence that all things will continue to work together for my good, and that God will answer petitions according to His will and good pleasure. I do not know what the future holds, but I do know Who holds the future. My purpose is to know Him, and to make Him known. I have witnessed His goodness and grace. I am enjoying my life.

My prayer for each one who reads this book, is that you, too, will be led to reflect on the goodness of God in your life, and know the joy of surrendering to God's will, even in the uncertainties, disappointments and storm clouds of life. May you embrace His plans for your life and find that the pathway leads you to deeper hope, joy, and faith.

Precious thought - my Father knoweth!
In His love I rest,
For whate'er my Father doeth
must be always best;
Well I know the heart that planneth
naught but good for me,
Joy and sorrow interwoven –
love in all I see.
Oh to trust Him then more fully,
just to simply move
In the conscious calm enjoyment
of the Father's love,
Knowing that life's chequered pathway
leadeth to His rest;
Satisfied the way He taketh
must be always best.
(Author unknown)[16]

ACKNOWLEDGEMENTS

I owe an immense debt of gratitude to the late Professor Sir Howard A. Fergus, KBE, PhD., my former high school teacher, mentor, brother in Christ, and friend. I had recovered sufficiently to attend Sunday service following my life-saving surgery in 2022 and I had given a testimony of God's sovereign intervention in that situation. Sir Howard gently tapped my shoulder after the service, and said to me, "You must write your story." And so, I did. He believed in me and continuously encouraged me in my walk with Christ. He left for the realms of Glory before the completion of this book, but I hope to meet him there, and tell him all about it.

The Caribbean Neurosurgery Foundation's outreach visits to Montserrat and Antigua in April 2022 saved my life. Dr. Myron L. Rolle, founder and Chair of the CNF, team members Dr. William Butler and Dr. Michael Groff, along with Dr. Patrick Knight, Consultant Neurosurgeon, were providentially in the right place at the right time. They, along with the doctors and nurses based at the Glendon Hospital in Montserrat and the Sir Lester Bird Medical Centre in Antigua, were all used by God to fulfil His purpose in a pivotal moment in my life. This triggered the reflections that have resulted in this book. I am indebted to all of these outstanding doctors and nurses.

Nerissa Golden has continuously and consistently supported my writing journey and provided enormous assistance in editing this work. Her suggestions were excellent, apt and most valuable. So too were the advice and suggestions of Jacinta Thomas, Allan Martin, Oral Howes, Audrey Welds, Judy Murdoch, Lesley Roberts, Valerie Hodge, Sylvester Carrington and Bernice James who each read portions of this manuscript. Phyllis Thomas was an excellent proof-reader, thorough and detailed in her comments and suggestions, for which I am deeply grateful. As always, I benefitted from the advice and encouragement of Edwin Martin.

I also deeply appreciated the inspiration and advice shared by a number of fellow writers in the Authorpreneur Secrets Academy, who provided moral support and guidance. In particular, the individual consultations and resources offered by Cameka Ruth Taylor were powerfully instructive and motivating.

My heartfelt thanks to all. To God be the Glory!

NOTES

1. Tison, R. (2015) "History and the Biblical Worldview". History and Government Faculty Publications 166, https://digitalcommons.cedarville.edu/history_and_government_publications/166/

2. Bridges, J. (2016) Trusting God. Colorado, USA, NavPress, 18.

3. Calvin, J. (2012). "John Calvin's Commentaries On The Psalms 119 - 150 (Annotated Edition)". Bavaria, Germany. Jazzybee Verlag p.166

4. Johns Hopkins Medicine. *Cerebrospinal Fluid (CSF) Leak,* https://www.hopkinsmedicine.org/health/conditions-and-diseases/cerebrospinal-fluid-csf-leak

5. Cleveland Clinic. *Cerebrospinal (CSF) Fluid Leak.* https://my.clevelandclinic.org/health/diseases/16854-cerebrospinal-fluid-csf-leak

6. Rolle, M. (2022) *The 2% Way.* USA, Zondervan.

7. Caribbean Neurosurgery Foundation, Inc. https://www.caribbeannf.org/

8. Portions of Chapter One were published earlier as part of an online article by Golden, N., in Discover Montserrat, 01

August, 2022, "Perfect Timing: How Myron Rolle's Caribbean Neurosurgery Foundation Helped Montserrat's Ann Marie Dewar", https://discovermni. com/2022/08/01/perfect-timing-caribbean-neurosurgery-foundation-helped-montserrats-ann-marie-dewar/

9. Sheridan, R. (1993) "From chattel to wage slavery in Jamaica, 1740-1860" in Twaddle, M. (Ed) *The Wages of Slavery: From Chattel Slavery to Wage Labour in Africa, the Caribbean and England.* London, Routledge.

10. Tutu, Desmond. (September 7, 1986) Address at his enthronement as Anglican Archbishop of Cape Town, https://www.azquotes.com/quote/298485

11. Gabriel, C.H. (1905). "He Lifted Me". Public Domain.

12. McTell, Ralph. (1969) "Streets of London". *Spiral Staircase* (Album). Transatlantic.

13. Historic St Kitts – "Edward Margetson", www.historicstkitts. kn/people/edward-margetson

14. Stuart, Victoria (1820-1915) "In the Shadow of the Highest". Public Domain.

15. Spurgeon, C. H. "Morning and Evening". (Updated Edition September 26, 2003), Wheaton, Illinois. Crossway.

16. "Precious thought – my Father knoweth". Author unknown, identified only by initials L.W. Public Domain.

ABOUT THE AUTHOR

Ann Marie Dewar OBE, is an educator and freelance training designer and facilitator who lives and works on the Caribbean island of Montserrat. As a musician, choral director, creole poet and costume maker, she has also been involved in the performing arts, locally, regionally and internationally. Her productive and successful career has spanned more than five decades, and she has received several awards for her services to Montserrat in education, culture and public service.

She is also the author of *Wha Marmie Say*, a collection of poetry in the native language of Montserrat.